Myself When Young

The Shaping of a Writer

Daphne du Maurier

G.K. HALL & CO.

Boston, Massachusetts

1978

Library of Congress Cataloging in Publication Data

Du Maurier, Daphne, Dame, 1907 -
    Myself when young.

    Large print ed.
    1. Du Maurier, Daphne, Dame, 1907 -   — Biography —
Youth.   2.   Authors, English — 20th century — Biography.
3.   Large type books.   I.   Title.
[PR6007.U47Z52   1978]   823'.9'12   [B]   78-14272
ISBN 0-8161-6611-0

Published in Large Print by arrangement with
Doubleday & Company, Inc.

Set in Photon 18 pt Crown

Myself when young did eagerly
  frequent
Doctor and Saint, and heard
  great argument
About it and about: but evermore
Came out by the same door as in
  I went.

Omar Khayyam

Contents

Author's Note

All autobiography is self-indulgent. Approaching my seventieth birthday, I find that I forget what happened a week ago but have a vivid memory of childhood days and the awkward age of adolescence, much of the latter period recorded in the diaries which I kept from the year 1920, when I was twelve, until I married in 1932. These diaries were intended for my personal reading, and it never occurred to me then that in late middle age, half a century afterwards, I should find them revealing, even nostalgic, and that they might interest not only my immediate family and my friends but others too — those who have asked me, from time to time, what made me choose writing as a career.

The following pages will, I hope, give them the answer. They cover my thoughts, impressions and actions from the age of three until I was twenty-five, after my first novel had been published. I was still uncertain of myself, naïve and immature, and readers looking for deep thoughts and words of wisdom will be disappointed. It is for this reason that I have called the book MYSELF WHEN YOUNG: THE SHAPING OF A WRITER. If it brings a smile to those of my contemporaries who also possess long memories, and at the same time encourages young writers, as unsure of themselves as I was once, to try their hand, then the record will not have been set down in vain.

24, Cumberland Terrace

We passed under the archway and came to the house at the end of the small court, on the right-hand side. There were steps leading up to the white front door, and the bell had to be rung so that the nurse could be helped to lift the pram up the steps and into the hall. The nurse was dressed in grey, and she wore a black bonnet on her head with a veil stretched tightly across her face. Ellison, the parlourmaid, wore a cream-coloured uniform, and she had a frilly cap and apron. They chatted a moment, exclaiming over the weight of the pram, while the baby within peered up at them, rosy-cheeked, smiling. Angela and I marched inside. Then I saw, to my dismay, coats and hats in the hall, and from the drawing room to the left of the long narrow entrance came the sound of laughter and talking. This meant there were people to lunch. We should be summoned later to say how do you do and to shake hands. Angela turned enquiringly to the parlourmaid, not minding, but I hurried upstairs to be out of the way, while Nurse lifted Baby from the pram.

The stairs conquered, I paused on the first-floor landing and looked over my shoulder down to the hall. Doors were opening. The talking was louder. I turned quickly to the right, and putting my hand on the banister pulled my way up our own short twisting flight of stairs to the nursery floor. There was a gate, standing open. Beyond was safety. I ran at once into the day nursery, the familiar warmth and smell of it bringing intense relief: here were the doll's house, the toy cupboard with two shelves — one for Angela, one for me — the cretonne-covered toy box, an old armchair that could be turned at will into a large ship wrecked at sea, and so into the wider part of the room with the table set for lunch, the fire burning behind the high brass guard and the wide window overlooking Albany Street and the barracks.

"Now then, no dawdling, hat and coat off, and hands washed before lunch."

The nurse had reached the top of our stairs with Baby. But I wanted to look down into Albany Street. The Life Guards might be coming back from their outing, breastplates gleaming, plumes proudly waving from their helmets. It was the bugle call that used to awaken us every morning, in the little room we shared, Angela and I, once I was promoted from the night nursery across the passage after Baby was born.

Tra-la-la, tra-la-la, tra-la-la-la.
Tra-la-la, tra-la-la, tra-la-la-la.
Tra-la-la, tra-la-la, tra-la-la
LAAAAA!

Nurse said it was called Reveille, but I knew what the bugle was saying. It said:

Bring in your horses and give them
to drink,

3

Bring in your horses and give them
   to drink,
Bring in your horses and give them
   to DRINK!

Such groomings there must be, such polishings of brass, such clatterings of hoofs, such quenching of thirst from the great troughs inside the barracks. It made something to think about before getting-up time, and having to dress in the cold bedroom, and going through to the night nursery to be washed and have teeth cleaned and, worst of all, the beastly rags pulled out of my hair which were put there to make it curl, though they never did.

Breakfast would follow. "Now, don't mess about with your spoon. Eat up your porridge." I did not like porridge. It made me feel sick. Lumpy, slimy, horrid. "If you were a little poor child always hungry you would be glad to eat your porridge." But I wasn't a little poor child, and saying that didn't make me eat it up. I wished the poor child could have it, not me.

"I don't care."

4

This was rude, and I might be punished for it. Made to stand in the corner, perhaps, and so not have to eat the porridge. But the nurse, whose name was Nurse Rush and who had replaced the much-loved nanny — we were not told why — contented herself with a snub.

"Don't Care was made to care,
Don't Care was hung,
Don't Care was put in a pot,
And cooked till he was done."

I thought for a moment, then poked once more at the porridge. Who was Don't Care? I wondered. Not a poor child. No, he sounded more like a little old man, rather tubby, who lived alone in a hut, and then some cruel people came and put him in this great black pot and hung it over a fire, which made a sizzling noise. Poor Don't Care . . . Did he scream? Or did some nice person come and rescue him? What happened next? But they never told you. Grownups started something interesting and would not finish. If you asked they said, "That will do now,"

5

which was the end of it.

Don't Care was made to care. I was on his side. And he became real, like the boy in *Reading Steps,* which I was trying to master. "Dan Ran To The Man." But why did Dan run to the man? Was somebody after him? Was he being chased by a wolf? "Meg Had A Sore Leg." Silly thing, perhaps she had fallen down, and then made a fuss. I saw her sitting on her bed and crying. "Ben Had A Fat Hen." He must have found it hard to hold, and then I expect it squawked, and flew out of his arms, and went fluttering off into a farmyard. If only I could read the longer words in the end pages they might tell me more about Dan and Meg and Ben, but the letters in these words were all joined together, not like the big letters.

I liked H. It was a gate, over which I could climb. And A was a swing I could sit on. B was a fat loaf. And G was a half-round like C, but had a little seat. One day soon the big letters would join on to the small letters and I should understand each one, and be able to read the writing in books and not just look at pictures. And

6

then, and then . . .

"Do you want to go somewhere?"

"No."

"Then what are you wriggling for?"

I don't know. . . . I was thinking of "Dan Ran To The Man" and what might have happened, and it made me excited, but they don't understand, and she drags me to the night nursery, and pulls down my knickers, and makes me sit on the chamber pot, and this is the most shaming thing of all — not even down to the bathroom, but stuck there, on the pot, like Baby. And the pot is too small. I spill what I do.

Then, suddenly, it's not after breakfast but after lunch (which also made me feel sick, those horrid greens and the rice pudding), and "Hurry up, now, you're to go downstairs and say how do you do."

Hands and face scrubbed, hair brushed, and down we go to the dreaded dining room. Angela is beaming, why doesn't she mind? Baby is smiling too, she is being carried so she is safe. The dining-room door is opened. The ladies are all at lunch. Lots of them. They all wear hats, which makes it worse. Even M* has a hat, giving her an unfamiliar look. Nurse Rush puts Baby in her arms, and Baby coos. The ladies all turn and look at us.

"Oh, aren't they *sweet?*"

But we're not sweet. At least, I'm not. Angela may be, prancing up to each lady in turn and shaking hands, and Baby, being given sugar from the coffee tray, but I am Don't Care, and Dan, and I hate them all, and when they suddenly get up from the table to go into the drawing room they are much too tall, they speak too loudly, they laugh too much, and it's always the same. Grownups are too big, too noisy, and worse besides they want to kiss me. I turn my face away.

"Oh, she's shy."

I'm not shy. I hate you, that's all. And I don't want to be kissed. I start tearing at my nails.

"Ah-ha! I can see a little girl who bites her nails."

"Yes, she will do it. We've tried bitter

---

* To avoid constant repetition of the names "Daddy" and "Mummy," seldom used today, I refer to my parents throughout as D and M.

aloes, but it doesn't stop her."

M shakes her head reproachfully. She pops another piece of coffee sugar into Baby's mouth. P'raps if they gave me sugar and not bitter aloes . . . Then they are all in the drawing room, still talking, still laughing, and when nobody is looking I run out of the room and upstairs, away to the safe nursery, and here at least they won't follow. Even Nurse Rush must be down below with Ellison and Alice the cook in the basement kitchen, also talking, also laughing.

I go to the window and look out over the rooftops, stretching forever. One house, painted red, attracts me. Why is it red? Who lives there? It's on its own, not friends with the other houses. I shall pretend it's mine, and that I live there alone. No porridge, no greens, no rice pudding, no feeling sick. I shall have a sword, like Peter Pan, and fight, if anyone comes. If only I could fly, but I can't, and anyway the nursery here is safe.

Was it now, humped at the table with a piece of paper and a pencil, struggling with pothooks, that I tried to put thoughts on paper, at four years old, so that when Miss Torrance, the governess, came to teach us later, and asked me if I could write, I turned to her and said, "Yes, I have written a book"?

"What is it called?"

"It's called *John, in the Wood of the World*."

It was not true, of course. I could barely turn pothooks into capitals, let alone form sentences to write a book. So why say it? Showing off, no doubt. But what made me choose such a title? I do not know. The hero of the nonexistent story was evidently lost, surrounded by trees, and whether he found his way to the light or remained in darkness I shall never discover.

Miss Torrance accepted the myth without scolding, however, and soon took her place amongst those grown-ups who were kind and understanding, and did not swoop to kiss, or, if they did, might be accepted. Like Little Granny, M's own mother, with her merry smile and chirpy ways, who was never, never cross. Like Aunt Billy, M's sister, my godmother, who was jolly and always in a good mood too. Like dear nanny, who had left soon after Baby grew bigger. Staring down at her, after she had said good-bye and passed through the nursery gate, I saw that she was crying, blowing her nose into her handkerchief. That was a puzzle. Grown-up people did not cry. Nor, on the other hand, should they behave with lack of dignity. There was one moment of everlasting shame, deeply imprinted on my mind about this time, when we were staying in the country, and M and Aunt Billy came out into the garden where I was playing, and they carried skipping ropes. Suddenly they both took the pins out of their hair and let the hair flow upon their shoulders, and then they jumped up and down, skipping, as children might do. I felt myself go scarlet. I bent down to the ground, not to see them, and began to search for pebbles in the gravel path. The lower I bent the more they skipped and laughed. Were they doing it on purpose? It was terrible to think of the loose hair and the jumping feet. They had changed from safe people into strangers.

Hide me, hide me . . .

A succession of nurses took the place of the loved nanny. Cross Nurse Rush, grumpy Nurse H'm-H'm (we called her this because she was forever humming), Nurse Bun, who was fat and liked her meals, then a string of Norland nurses in brown caps and bonnets. I wonder why they came and went so fast? We were not naughty children. We did as we were told. Perhaps M was too particular, and found fault with them over trifles. We never asked. We shall never know.

Walks became longer with the Norlands. Instead of the Broad Walk in Regent's Park, bordering the Zoo — exciting this, because the wild animals were near — we were marched to Park Square Gardens some way off, and I soon saw the reason for this, for the current Norland nurse met friends, and once inside the gardens, which were enclosed by tall railings, so that you had to enter with a key, she would sit with the other nurses in a cosy shelter out of the cold wind, and they drank hot cocoa out of a Thermos flask, and ate biscuits. Baby, lucky thing, was snug and warm in her pram beside them.

"Now then, run along and play."

I did not want to play. My feet were frozen. My boots were too small. I wanted to sit in the shelter and be warm with them. No use, though. And for some reason Angela was not with me. She must have been doing lessons at home with Miss Torrance. Lessons that were too advanced for me.

"Run along. Do as you're told."

In the Wood of the World, indeed. Out into the cold air, along a wide path, towards a clearing where there was a sand pit. But here was the dread, for the friendly children, who sometimes played there, might be absent, and instead of their smiling faces I would see my enemy, waiting, lurking, his fair hair cropped short, his blue eyes without a gleam. He ran across to me at once and kicked me hard. I did not answer. I did not cry. His name was John Poynton. He was the scourge of Park Square Gardens, and the other children knew it too. He was seven years old.

"You're French, aren't you? You're a stupid Frenchie."

No reply. He kicked me again. "Go on. Say your name."

"Daphne."

"Surname."

"Du Maurier."

"There. What did I tell you? Stupid Frenchie."

He called over his shoulder and another boy, smaller than himself, came out of the bushes. He was wearing a pink coat and a big black felt hat turned up all round. His name was Lionel. He was John Poynton's toady.

"Now look, Frenchie. We're going away, but you have to stand here without moving until we come back. If you move, we shall know."

They disappeared. In the distance I could see grown-ups walking, but they did not glance in my direction. No one could help. I obeyed orders. I did not move. In about five minutes, an eternity, the boys returned.

"You *did* move," shouted John Poynton in triumph. "We were watching, and we saw you."

"I didn't move," I told him.

"Lying Frenchie. This is what you get, then."

And he began to kick me harder than before, his companion laughing. Whether I flung out at him, what happened next, I don't know, but somehow I must have escaped and run back to the safety of the warm shelter, where the nurses were still chatting, still drinking their hot cocoa, but I wasn't crying and I didn't tell them. It would have been no use. They would not have believed me, any more than the enemy John Poynton had believed me. Here was something that was hard to accept, far less understand, at five years old. In the Wood of the World you're on your own.

Not always, though. For now that I could read properly, to myself, not slowly and aloud at lesson time, the people in books became companions. The baby books first, where the words were easy. Tom Kitten, Mrs. Tiggy-Winkle, Tabitha Twitchet, Peter Rabbit, I was soon word-perfect, the animals were real. There was that terrible rat with his rolling pin, upstairs in an empty room. There was angry Mr. McGregor. Sinister Mr. Tod the fox with his bushy tail. And why did Jeremy Fisher make me shiver when he knocked, leering, at Mrs. Twitchet's door? Little books led to bigger books, but they had to be exciting, they had to have adventures. Not fairy tales, these were silly.

Sometimes, for a treat, when Angela and I went downstairs to the drawing room after tea, M would read to us aloud. The book was *Naughty Sophia*. It was all about an archduchess who was also a child. For some reason she went to live with a peasant family, and she made friends with a boy called Hans.

And another book, *The Snow Queen*. The Queen was wicked. She drove through the snow in an icy chariot taking a little boy with her, so that his blood would turn to icicles. His name was Kay. He had a friend called Gerda, who finally rescued him. As I listened I became each child in turn, first Kay, then Gerda, and when M had finished and it was time to go upstairs to bed, and M pretended to chase us, it was not funny at all, I saw her as the Snow Queen, and I was frightened. It was much worse than being kicked by John Poynton. If I could turn into Kay, and M could become the Snow Queen, then who was I really, where did I belong? The Snow Queen was an enemy, like that other Queen, the stepmother, who looked into a mirror and asked it:

"Mirror, mirror, on the wall,
Who is the fairest of us all?"

One day the mirror answered that the most beautiful one was her stepdaughter, and the Queen decided to kill her. Evil women were more terrible than evil men. I would rather be the Babes in the Wood murdered by the robbers than Kay, with his blood turned to icicles. Witches were worse than wizards. Wizards were just old men with cloaks and a wand. But witches did not have to be old, they were sometimes beautiful, and then you could not tell until it was too late.

One thing was certain. D was not a wizard. We had to be quiet in the morning because he slept late and the nurseries were over their bedrooms, but when he was awake and having breakfast in bed, wearing a green flannel coat over his pyjamas, and we went to say good morning, his face would be clean and smiling, he smelt good, and he was never in a bad mood. He smacked me once, when I put out my tongue at our nanny, but only the once. And when he came up to the nursery to see us and say good night — he was seldom at home in the daytime — he was always funny, and made us laugh.

Sometimes we would go to fetch him from the theatre, the place where he went during the day. Bob, the stage-doorkeeper, would smile down on us from his stool, and there would be the musty theatre smell, with stage hands moving about and shifting the scenery. Stairs to the dressing room, stage entrance on the left, stairs to the other dressing rooms on the right. And Poole, D's dresser, who had a rather red face and mumbled as he spoke, hovering at the entrance to D's dressing room. D would be laughing there too, wiping the stuff off his face, and somehow I knew and understood that in the theatre he pretended to be a different person, and that was why he put the stuff on his face and changed his clothes, and all the people waiting and watching behind the big curtain were excited because of it. We were not taken in, though, as they were. No matter how much he pretended, it was really D all the time, so there was nothing to fear. With M I was not quite so sure. She might have been the Snow Queen in disguise.

I saw why D liked to dress up and pretend to be someone else; I began to do it myself, and so did Angela, and even Baby, who could walk by now and was called Jeanne, could join in the play. Miss Torrance, who still came in the mornings to give us lessons, suggested to M that we should perform in front of visitors. It was a strange thing, but the very act of putting on fancy dress and becoming another person stopped the feeling of panic when visitors came. There they would sit, in rows of chairs in the drawing room, and the double doors leading to the dining room would be closed, then suddenly they would be rolled back, and Angela and I would be standing there, like D behind his curtain at the theatre, and the visitors did not crowd round us, they just sat in their chairs and clapped.

Angela was very good. She sang "Au Clair de la Lune" and recited in French too, but the best time was when Miss Torrance made her a gold crown out of paper, and she had a cloak, and her name was King Henry V. I had to come on first, which I did not mind, because I also had a cloak, a short one, and a velvet hat, and I was someone called the Earl of Westmoreland. Miss Torrance told me to look very serious, which I did, putting my hand up to my chin as I walked slowly up and down, and though I did not understand exactly what I was saying I knew that the Earl of Westmoreland must be very worried, so I felt worried for him, we were one and the same.

"O that we now had here

But one ten thousand of those men
in England
That do no work today!''

In a moment the double doors were opened and Angela, with the gold crown on her head, stepped in and stood beside me. She was smiling proudly.

"What's he that wishes so?
My cousin Westmoreland? — No, my
fair cousin:
If we are marked to die, we are
enow
To do our country loss. . . .''

She went on talking for a long time, getting more and more proud, stamping her foot, looking from right to left. There was something about the feast of Crispin, and I had to stay quiet, still rather worried, and I felt sorry for the Earl of Westmoreland, who was me, because he could not interrupt and shout, "Huzza!" or "Nay, nay!" In fact, when Angela with a great flourish cried:

"And gentlemen in England now
   a-bed
Shall think themselves accurs'd they
   were not here,
And hold their manhood cheap while
   any speaks
That fought with us upon Saint
   Crispin's Day"

it was the end of the speech, and everyone clapped, and we both bowed. Miss Torrance never told me what the Earl of Westmoreland did next, and if he stopped being worried about the ten thousand men who had no work in England.

I wondered about it a bit, and then I forgot. The winter was over, and soon it would be time to go to the country, for every year from May until August we would go to some other house that was not really ours, with the nurse and the maids, and M and D not always there because of the theatre. One year it was Denham, the next Croxley Green, then Slyfield — Slyfield with the river Mole running through the garden, Slyfield with the big cedar tree on the lawn, Slyfield with the farm buildings and the farm animals alongside.

Here at last was freedom. No longer the same walks day after day, the sound of buses in Albany Street, being quiet in the early morning, the routine that never varied; but instead space all around. We could run outside when we wanted and where we wanted, nurses did not scold so much in the country, maids were jollier, M did not wear a hat at lunch and say, "Stop biting your nails" in that reproachful voice, Angela and I did not squabble. The country . . . the country . . .

"She's a different child altogether out of London," I heard someone say. Of course I was different. Here there were fields, trees, birds, animals. The farm men next door, Arthur and Tom, used to lift us on to their great horses and take us round the yard. "I'm going to marry Arthur," whispered Angela. She was nine by now, and thought about these things. Arthur was dark and handsome. This I could see. But at six I did not fancy Tom, he was too old.

Miss Torrance had been left behind in London, and Miss Bishop came every morning from the village of Stoke d'Abernon to give us lessons. Henry V and the Earl of Westmoreland were no more. *The Pilgrim's Progress* had me enslaved. I was Christian. I did everything he did. I copied his actions. On our walks by the river Mole we would come to a little gate and this was the wicket gate through which Christian passed in the story. The muddied fields after rain could be the Slough of Despond, bushes and trees Vanity Fair, and the river Mole itself the great divide at the end: "And all the trumpets sounded for him on the other side."

Miss Bishop had sisters, and sometimes we went to tea at the parsonage, for their father was a clergyman. After tea they would take us down the garden and show us a small circle of flowers, neatly arranged, and in the centre a note, with tiny writing upon it.

"It's a fairy ring," said the Miss Bishops, "and the fairies have written to you. Look, they know your names are

Angela and Daphne.''

Angela, eyes wide open in wonder, smiled delightedly. I stared at the circle. I must pretend to be pleased too, but the trouble was I did not believe them. I felt sure they had made the fairy ring themselves, and had written the note. Besides, if the truth be told, I did not believe in fairies. Tinker Bell was all very well in *Peter Pan,* but I knew the light that danced about on the stage was really shone by one of the theatre men.

Miss Bishop read the note. It said the fairies hoped we would come again. ''There! Isn't that kind of them?''

This pleased Angela. It pleased the Miss Bishops too. But I was not deceived.

''They wrote it themselves,'' I said after we got back.

''They wouldn't! Of course it was real.'' Angela was indignant.

I shook my head. ''It's the sort of thing grownups do.''

I still believed in Father Christmas, and yet . . . How did he manage to get down everybody's chimneys all in the one night? It just couldn't be done. And supposing he didn't . . . supposing it wasn't true . . . ? I remembered finding a net stocking full of toys hidden under a cushion in M's morning room at Cumberland Terrace. Why was it there? If something was not true, why make it up in the first place? But then, here was the puzzle. Stories in books were not true. The person who wrote the book made them up. Somehow, that did not matter. *Pilgrim's Progress* was a story. It did not really happen. That was all right. But if fairies were just invented to deceive children, and Father Christmas too, what about the picture in my prayer book that my godmother Billy had given me, with God looking out of a great cloud in the sky, staring down at the boy Jesus, who was standing with his mother Mary and his father Joseph? If Father Christmas was supposed to live in the sky and drive reindeer on Christmas Eve, sleeping the rest of the year, why didn't God let him carry the baby Jesus and drop him down the stable chimney at Bethlehem when he was born on Christmas Day? Was Father Christmas meant to be God's brother?

"Don't be so silly. What a stupid question."

It was all very well. People looked awkward when you kept asking why, why, why. . . . No Father Christmas might mean no God. And anyway, how could God balance up in the sky in all those clouds, forever and ever, now and again booming down messages to the Children of Israel, who often disobeyed them?

The Bible stories were good. I liked Cain better than Abel, and Esau better than Jacob, and Joshua was a true hero, blowing his trumpet round the walls of Jericho. Best of all was David, slinging a stone at Goliath. Why wasn't I born a boy? They did all the brave things. Fought all the battles. If I had been a boy I could have fought John Poynton and beaten him. As it was I had to make do with pretending, tuck my dress into my knickers, find a stick and wave it like a sword. Angela did not mind being a girl. In our make-up games she took the part of a girl, and would throw open the window of the Wendy house in the garden calling, "Save me, save me!" Then bravely I would slash at the bushes, our enemies, and run to her rescue.

"Come along in, it's time for tea."

Just as things were getting exciting. . . . Even at Slyfield the washing of hands, the combing of hair, the ritual of grace. "For what I am about to receive, the Lord make me truly thankful." Thankful for bread and butter, which must be eaten before the jam. Why? Get it over. The Lord wasn't listening. And it was summer out of doors, and we could go on playing once tea was finished. But when it came to bedtime, and the sword was laid aside, then things were not so good. The staircase at Slyfield was not straight up like the stairs at Cumberland Terrace. The hall at Slyfield was larger, darker, somehow, and the staircase was wide, turning to a broad landing above. Angela, being older, was allowed to stay up later. She would be down in the drawing room with M. Jeanne was already in bed. So the stairs must be climbed alone. They gave me a queer feeling.

"Yes," someone had said when we first

went, "it's a very old house, they say the site is mentioned in Domesday. And in Tudor times Queen Elizabeth slept here."

Domesday had an ominous sound. And was Queen Elizabeth another Snow Queen waiting for me on the murky landing above? A sword was no use now. Up, up, one step at a time, my heart thumping, while the staircase creaked. A picture of a man on the wall. I must not look at him, or something terrible would happen. The landing at last, and pushing open a door I was through to a place of safety, I could hear voices, I was somehow in the bedroom that we used as a night nursery and Jeanne was there in her cot. Nurse was tucking her up. Fear vanished. Domesday was no more. Queen Elizabeth had gone. Yet later, bath over, teeth brushed, rags in my hair and the light turned out, I was not so sure. The staircase would still be dark, the picture hanging on the wall, shadows on the landing. Where had they all gone, the people who lived at Slyfield once? And where was I then? Who was I now?

It was next year, late August, and we were all in Wales. A house called Plas Gwinfryn, near Llanbedr. D had a holiday from the theatre, so the house was filled with uncles, aunts, cousins, friends — D liked a lot of people around him all the time — and we children, because of the crowd, lived in a cottage at the end of the garden. This was much nicer than being in the house because it was more free, and we felt the cottage was ours, while the house was theirs. Funny, how we seemed to be on different sides. Them and us. Or was it only I who felt this? Angela was much more friendly, and now that she could run around and talk so was Jeanne, with her curly hair and rosy cheeks. But though I was seven, and growing fast so that grownups no longer seemed so tall, they were still Them, different, apart; I could sometimes tell by watching who could be counted as friend and trustworthy, and who could be ignored.

You could never be quite sure of any of them, even relations. Although I liked D better than M (which must never be said, even to myself), M's mother, our Little

Granny, was, so I thought, more lovable than Big Granny, mother of D. Big Granny was tall and rather solemn, and though she was very kind and gave us better toys at Christmas than Little Granny ever did, somehow I never felt quite at ease when we went to see her at her flat in Portman Mansions.

It was the same with the aunts. Godmother Billy, M's sister, was like one of ourselves, and though she scolded sometimes it wasn't the kind of scolding that sank in. Two of D's sisters were now dead, and only Aunt May was left. People said I looked like her, which I couldn't see at all, because she was dark, going grey, and had brown eyes, and when one kissed her the bones in her cheek felt sharp. She was said to have "nerves." She had a dog called Poolo who smelt. Once, when we were staying at Ramsgate with Big Granny, who had a house there when she wasn't in London, I was going downstairs by myself, one step at a time, and singing, or rather humming, staring at the model of the tugboat on a shelf which, if I could only touch it, would be the greatest of all possible treats, when suddenly a door on the landing was thrown open and Aunt May came out, her eyes blazing.

"How *dare* you make such a noise when I am resting?" she shouted.

I stared, mouth open. I stood quite still. Then without another word she went back into her room and shut the door. The encounter was a shock. I told no one. However pleasant, clever and amusing she turned out to be in after years, that memory remained, indelible, and I always felt that she was fonder of Angela and Jeanne than she was of me. Was it because of the meeting on the stairs?

Cousins were another matter. All the cousins on D's side of the family were boys, older than us, and therefore to be admired and envied, even loved. George, Jack, Peter, Michael, Nico . . . Had I known, at the age of five, six, seven, how the Greeks felt about their Olympian gods, I would have shared their sentiments. Jack, as a midshipman, was, so I thought, everything in life that I could never be. He had climbed nearly to the top of the great cedar tree on Slyfield lawn. I had seen him in uniform. He had once called at Cumberland Terrace just to see me and present me with some sweets. Yet to enter a room and be told, "Cousin Jack is here," so filled me with anguish that I thought I should die. Perhaps, like Aunt May, I had "nerves."

There were no girl cousins on D's side of the family, but M's brother, Uncle Willie, had two daughters just our age, Cynthia and Ursula, and they joined our happy circle down in the cottage at Plas Gwinfryn. Despite the mist and rain we enjoyed ourselves, although baby Derek, son of grown-up Cousin Geoffrey and Cousin Dorothy, cried a lot, but the friends and relations up at the big house seemed, towards mid-August, to be under strain. They kept talking about a war. One day, when for some reason or other we children were having lunch with the grownups, and not on our own at the cottage as we usually did, everyone sitting round the dining-room table, the telephone went, and Cousin Dorothy came bursting into the room. "Germany's started fighting Russia,'' she said. Silence. Then they all began talking at once. Why were they so concerned? I wondered. (In fact, Belgium had already been invaded and the French had suffered heavy losses; the news broken by Cousin Dorothy must have referred to the start of the fighting in East Prussia, where the victory of General Ludendorff over the Russians at Tannenberg took place between August 28th and 31st.)

I understood not a word of what was being discussed. My knowledge of geography was limited. Miss Torrance had told me about the Earl of Westmoreland's anxiety upon St. Crispin's Day, and Miss Bishop had whipped up enthusiasm for the pilgrim Christian, but why the fever now? One thing was plain. Everybody round the dining table hated, loathed the Germans, whoever they were. It was time someone spoke in their defence. I waited for a momentary pause in the torrent of conversation, and seized my chance.

"I like the Germans," I said. "I would like to have a German to tea with me here today."

Everyone stared. Perhaps this had been my real motive. Then M, from the head of the table, rounded upon me, her colour high.

"You *stupid* little girl," she said. "How dare you talk about things you don't understand?"

I was instantly silent. People looked away, and began to talk about something else. Instinctively I knew that what I had said was foolish, ignorant, and I felt ashamed, and yet . . . there was a sense of secret satisfaction that I had somehow scored against the grown-up world.

Whether Germany fighting Russia brought panic to the household, or whether the lease of Plas Gwinfryn had come to an end, I shall never know, but in a few days we were all back in Cumberland Terrace. And our world began to change.

Soon there were soldiers everywhere. Not our Life Guards on horses with their waving plumes, but soldiers on foot, wearing khaki, marching down Albany Street and through Regent's Park. They sang and whistled, and people in the street waved and shouted. I forgot about wanting to be a midshipman like Cousin Jack, and insisted that I must be a soldier too. I was given a khaki uniform for Christmas. The leggings, or puttees as they were called, were hard to put on my legs and I couldn't wrap them properly, but the soldier's hat was superb. Big Granny came to lunch and said I must knit. She would teach me to knit a scarf for the real soldiers. I fumbled with the awful needles to please her, then hid them when she had gone.

Then, suddenly, things started to get sad. D's only brother, our uncle Guy, was a soldier, and he had to go to the war. We all went to see him off at Waterloo Station. There were crowds of soldiers, and the soldiers' relations, all walking along the platform. Big Granny was with us, and she kissed Uncle Guy as he got into the train, and then he leant out of the window and waved to her, and the train was gone. I saw Big Granny turn and put out her hand, and she crumpled up on the platform and fell, with everyone crowding around her, and I heard M say, "Oh, God, she's fainted." A porter came with a glass of water, and I saw Big Granny lying there, in her long black dress and cape, her bonnet pushed back from her white hair, while D knelt beside her. I kept thinking how much Big Granny loved Uncle Guy, and that she had fainted because he had gone away to the war.

It was sadder still some months later, when Big Granny became really ill and died. And then Cousin George, who was twenty-one, was killed at the front. And one day, as I was walking down the stairs at Cumberland Terrace, Angela came out of D and M's bedroom, and she was crying. "Uncle Guy has been killed," she said. He was her godfather, but I had a part in him too, his birthday had been the same as mine, May 13th. There was a photograph of him in a newspaper with writing underneath. It said, "A patriot, alike with sword and with pen." I asked M what it meant, and she told me Uncle Guy had written a play some years ago called *An Englishman's Home*, all about Germany invading England; he knew it might happen, and there would be war one day. He was a very brave soldier, she said, his men loved him, and now that Big Granny was dead, and Uncle Guy, poor D had none of his family left but Aunt May.

I had not realised until then that grown-up people could be unhappy, that they could cry. I did not want to think about it. But we could wear black bands round our arms when we went out, and the children in the Park Square Gardens came up and asked, "Who have you lost in the war?" and we said, "Uncle Guy, and Cousin George," and added, "Big Granny," for good measure. This somehow made us feel important, and therefore better.

The war went on, with the soldiers marching and singing, and we learnt some of their songs, like:

"Who were you with last night
    Out in the pale moonlight?
    It wasn't your sister,
    It wasn't your ma,
    Ah! Ah! Ah! Ah! Ah-Ah-Ah-AH!"

This last line had to be sung roguishly, wagging a finger in the air.

And there was another:

"Who-who-who's your lady friend,
Who's the little girlie by your side?
It isn't the one I saw you with at
Brighton,
Who-who-who's your lady friend?"

Singing these songs made us forget to be sad about Uncle Guy, and one day Angela told me that she had overheard someone tell Nurse Netta that in wartime everyone made eyes at the soldiers.

"What does it mean, making eyes?" I asked her.

"I think it's like this," Angela said, looking sideways out of the corner of her eyes.

We practised this awhile, and afterwards, when we were walking in Regent's Park, and saw soldiers coming towards us, we used to stare at them sideways, in a squinting sort of way, smiling at the same time. Angela said it was patriotic. But I don't think they noticed, which was disappointing.

One good thing was that the war had not

changed the routine of going to the country for the summer. This year, 1915, it was no longer Slyfield but a much smaller house, almost a cottage, called Soulsbridge, Chorley Wood. There was greater freedom here than ever before. M and D did not seem to come down quite so often, and we had meals in the kitchen. Angela did lessons every day with a family who lived across the common, and for the first time ever I was allowed to wander out of the garden and walk across the fields by myself, with one companion; this was the first dog we children had ever possessed, a West Highland terrier called Jock. He had devoted himself to me from the beginning, ever since I had crept down to the basement in Cumberland Terrace the morning he arrived and seen him standing there, tied to a chair. We looked at each other. Then he wagged his tail, and I knew.

The neighbouring farmer at Soulsbridge kept Highland cattle, wonderful beasts with shaggy coats and great horns. Immensely daring, Jock and I would approach them, stealthily, and before they lowered their massive heads to come towards us we would be off, and across the fields.

Now Angela was away most of the day Jeanne, at four years old, became my ally, adapting herself with surprising ease into the various characters from the books I read. Uncle Willie, M's brother, gave me *Treasure Island,* and from that moment a whole new world awaited me.

"Squire Trelawney, Doctor Livesey, and the rest of these gentlemen . . ." I soon had the first page by heart, myself playing the part of Jim Hawkins, with occasional lapses into Long John Silver. Jeanne would come tapping along the garden path as blind Pew while I crouched in an imaginary ditch, in the lane near the Admiral Benbow Inn. Jeanne understood little of her role, but this did not matter.

Other books followed. *The Wreck of the Grosvenor:* "There was every appearance of a southwesterly wind . . ." I was Edward Royle, the narrator, the young second mate, and if Jeanne could hardly bellow as the bully Captain Coxon at least she could shout, "Clew up the mainsail and furl it," and stamp her foot. "The biscuits are full of weevils, the pork stinks," I would mutter as we ate our lunch in the kitchen, Jeanne nodding vigorously, while Nurse Netta stared at us in consternation. But the book became rather silly towards the end, because Edward Royle, after the mutiny and the shipwreck, turned soppy over the passenger Mary Robertson. "I pressed my darling to me." No, this wouldn't do at all. I skipped all that part and went back to the mutiny.

It was not at Chorley Wood but at Cookham, where we were sent later in the war to escape the Zeppelin raids, that D presented us with a full edition, superbly illustrated, of Harrison Ainsworth. And now *Old St. Paul's* held prior place for demonstrations. "Bring out your dead . . . bring out your dead," I called, and Jeanne, from the bedroom window, would throw all the teddy bears down to where I stood in the garden below, the wheelbarrow a convenient death cart, and so off to the nearest flower bed which might serve as a temporary plague pit. A pity I could not draw a big cross on the garden door to show that the house was plague-ridden, but this would have caused trouble. Plasticine, bought at the village shop, was useful, though, for we could soften it in our hands and mould it to make "pustules," or plague spots, and then, ramming it on face, arms and chest, cry out that we were stricken, stagger, and fall to the ground.

The Tower of London gave even greater opportunity for invention. I knew every inch of the ground and precincts before we were first taken there, walked without hesitation to stand by Traitor's Gate, and then pointed out, correctly, the name of every tower commanding the walls. Had I not beheaded Jeanne, time and time again, on Tower Green? I knew the identical spot where the block had stood. "How nobly she walks to her death," I heard one of the maids whisper, when Tower Green had been the garden of the moment. Jeanne, strutting past, certainly made a moving figure, her curls pinned on the top of her head, while I, the axeman, waited, walking stick in hand —

the crook of the handle forming the axe —
and, as was the rightful custom, dropped
on one knee to ask her pardon before I
felled her with a single blow.

Angela always took the women's parts.
She was splendid as Bloody Mary, for
whom she vowed she had a real affection,
but the trouble with Angela, as the years
passed, was that she soon lost interest,
once a game had started, and would
suddenly say, "Oh, I don't think I want to
play after all," and wander off on some
ploy of her own. This would spoil the
carefully planned sequence of events, and
the plot must be altered in mid-
enactment. Jeanne showed more
enthusiasm and, being nearly four years
my junior, proved malleable to my
direction, switching from role to role, one
moment Gog the giant and the next
moment Xit the dwarf, but more often the
hapless victim of the executioner's axe. I
have no recollection of ever suffering that
hideous fate myself, though on occasion I
would stretch myself upon the rack, or
better still writhe, attacked by rodents, in
the notorious Rat Pit.

In 1916, however, with *Old St. Paul's* and *The Tower of London* still unread, a momentous change in our lives took place. We left Cumberland Terrace forever and moved to Hampstead. The nurseries on the top floor knew us no more. We should never again awaken to the bugles in Albany Street, look out over the rooftops, walk in Regent's Park, avoid John Poynton in Park Square Gardens. Nostalgia belongs to the middle years of life, and at forty-three D, with his mother, his two sisters and his beloved brother dead, believed that by moving to his birthplace, close to his boyhood home, he might in some indefinable fashion recapture them. As children we were, of course, unaware of any such sentiment. Twelve, nine and five, the future was all ours. A house with a large garden, where we could play all day without putting on hats and coats? Hampstead Heath about us to explore? Who cared about Cumberland Terrace?

I cannot even remember slamming the nursery door for the last time.

Cannon Hall

Our new home was altogether different. The night nursery, which Jeanne and I shared, had its own bathroom and lavatory. This was promotion indeed. No longer a nurse to supervise but a children's maid, whose orders we could disregard. The day nursery was on the other side of the house, and could be reached in three separate ways: by running down the imposing main staircase, going through the dining room, and running up a secondary staircase known as the green stairs; by running up the back staircase, which was outside the night-nursery door, along the white corridor on the second floor outside D and M's bedrooms, and so down the higher flight of the green stairs; and by crossing the first-floor landing and slipping through the double drawing room, which took about one minute.

These last two methods were unpopular with the grown-up world, but when they were out of the way a superb race could be set in motion between Jeanne and myself, one of us taking the first alternative, the other the second. I generally found the second the most successful. It was cheating to go through the drawing room. Besides, someone might be dusting there. Angela now had her own little bedroom, on the same floor as M and D, and was therefore superior. She did not join in the races.

I soon discovered that our lavatory window led on to a flat roof over the dustbins in the courtyard, and by climbing out of this window, and creeping along this same flat roof, one could drop down over the dustbins and reach the courtyard. This was promptly discouraged. A pity. It damped adventure.

The garden at the back of the house made up for this disappointment. First a

47

lawn, then, encircled by bushes, a parapet that looked down onto the lower garden several feet below, where there was a herbaceous border, and also vegetables. I would walk along the narrow parapet, eyes front, while Jeanne, below me in the lower garden, would try to climb up through it unseen, and so surprise me. This she seldom achieved. Making eyes at the soldiers in Regent's Park had not been wasted effort after all. There were also the coalshed and the woodshed, which in days gone by had been the old Hampstead lockup. So now we had a real prison — when the gardener was at his vegetables — to transform into a cell, its blackened walls and barred slit windows daunting to whichever of us was taking the part of prisoner at the time.

The furniture and pictures at Cumberland Terrace had made little impression on me, save for our own chairs, tables and toy cupboards in the nursery. Here at Cannon Hall it was another matter. Despite the war, or more likely because *The Ware Case* and *London Pride* — with D playing a cold-blooded murderer in the one and a Cockney costermonger in the other — proved very successful plays, no expense was spared in making the new home handsome, with furniture appropriate to its mid-Georgian period. "George III's physician used to live here," visitors would be told when they came to admire the house on Sundays.

Never mind George III, it was the pictures D bought to decorate the walls up the big staircase that fascinated me. They were not in period at all. Sad King Charles in profile came on the right-hand wall as one started to climb the stairs, and above him, stretching the whole width of the wall, was a great battle picture, which could be enacted again and again. Then, gazing down from the wall at the head of the stairs, Queen Elizabeth herself, and remembering her ghostly presence at Slyfield I treated her with respect.

Easier to perform were the characters in the many prints from Shakespeare's plays scattered about the house, mostly up the green staircase. Prince Hal standing with his foot on Harry Hotspur's crumpled form — naturally, I was Prince Hal and Jeanne Hotspur; Othello smothering Desdemona; Titania surrounded by fairies (Angela could oblige for this, since it was a girl's part); Macbeth confronting the witches; Cranmer bearing the baby Princess Elizabeth at her christening, accompanied by a retinue of nobles — the possibilities were endless. It was about this time that I must have discovered Lamb's *Tales from Shakespeare,* and so could match the stories to the pictures, and discover what they were all about. The verses beneath the pictures were from the plays.

> "O Harry, thou hast robbed me of
>   my youth . . ."

This would be Jeanne, lying on her back as Hotspur, and I would reply:

> "Fare thee well, great heart.
> Ill-weav'd ambition, how much art
>   thou shrunk!"

— which in Lamb's *Tales* was rather simpler to understand, but I got the message.

And now D would sometimes join our games and encourage us, quoting long passages from all the pictures which he seemed to know by heart, and he bought Jeanne and myself boxing gloves, and showed us how to box each other without hurting. This was followed by cricket — visitors on Sundays were obliged to join in — but it was never very popular with M, who would call out anxiously, "Now do be careful not to make a mess of the lawn."

D suddenly became a fund of stories about his own boyhood days in Hampstead. He would take us up to his old home, New Grove House, and although it now belonged to someone else we would stare up at it, and listen as he said, "There's the studio. That's where Papa drew every day, he never minded us children playing around him. And there, behind the wall, is the small garden. You've seen the picture he drew of us, pretending to be trains, with Aunt Trixie leading, and myself the baby at the end."

It all began to make sense. D as a child. Grandpapa — who died before Angela was born — with, D told us, a kind heart which made everyone love him, and a feeling for family that stretched to nephews, nieces, cousins and second cousins, so that any who needed help were not afraid to come to him, a man of very simple tastes unaffected by fame and fortune. Big Granny not white-haired then, but younger, handsome, smiling. We would turn away from New Grove House and he would point to Heath Mount, his first school, with schoolboys there still, wearing green caps. On to the White Stone Pond, where he used to sail a boat, into which Grandpapa had once jumped to save a drowning dog, whose owner tipped him for his pains.

"That's the walk he took every morning," D would go on. "He had to walk to a certain spot and touch a tree there with his walking stick. If he forgot it would be unlucky." And then, pointing to the fallen branch of what had once been a gnarled tree, he smiled and said, "Look, there's my armchair. I always called it my armchair and sat in it. It's still there."

"I'm going to sit in it too," I said, and ran along to the branch and climbed into it, and yes, it was exactly like a chair. D had sat there, as a boy, about my age. And now he was a man. Where had the boy gone? It was haunting, queer . . . Then, finally, the trek down to the parish churchyard where Grandpapa was buried, and Big Granny. Aunt Sylvia was in the grave alongside, and there was a memorial to George and another to Uncle Guy, and by this time D would have tears in his eyes, so that one looked away. We would stand there, silently, saying nothing, but D could never stay sad for long, and soon he would be laughing and joking again, the sadness forgotten, but the dead relations in their grave who had never meant very much to me gradually became real and all of them young, while the pictures that Grandpapa had drawn in the pages of *Punch* — we had volumes of them, in a bookcase — became suddenly full of meaning. It was easy to recognise who was who, which elegant lady in a drawing room was really Big Granny, which long-haired schoolgirl one of the aunts.

So dawned family interest, family pride, which was something quite other than clapping from a box in Wyndham's Theatre when the curtain went up and D was standing there, smiling, bowing his head, looking from right to left and then up to the gallery, which happened at the end of the play. This was just part of something I had always known, it had nothing to do with us children but belonged to the audience, the people down there and all around, whom we should never know, who were not "us."

Perhaps it was the sense of closeness to D that made one apprehensive when the air raids started and he was not yet home from the theatre. We would be awakened in the night nursery by the earsplitting siren, followed quickly by the crash of the Hampstead anti-aircraft gun, only a short distance away, near the White Stone Pond. This was worse than the siren, shaking the whole house, and Jeanne began to cry. "It's only a thunderstorm," said the maid who shared our room, but Harry Hotspur was not deceived, crying all the louder, and I watched the shivering maid, more frightened than we were, reach for her slippers and run from the room. The coward, I thought, the coward . . .

Then M in her dressing gown came to comfort us, with Angela, bearing a Thermos flask of hot chocolate, and biscuits, but the anxious expression on her face and a half glance at the curtained window was a sign that D was not yet home. What might happen to him on the long drive back up Haverstock Hill? It must have been this sense of fear which overwhelmed me when we had a sudden unexpected daylight raid, and were all in the hall about to descend into the little cupboard under the stairs for safety. The Hampstead gun exploded with even greater force than usual, and D, not yet dressed, standing in his pyjamas and jacket halfway up the stairs, said, "By Jove, they must be close overhead. I think I shall go up to the roof and watch."

In an agony of fear for him, never

experienced before or since, I stretched out my arms and cried, "Don't go . . . don't go . . . Don't ever leave me."

He stared at me, then looked at M. She said, "Gerald, *please.*"

Slowly he came downstairs and joined us in the hall, and soon we heard the blessed sound of the all clear. It must have been the memory of that moment which made watching him act Will Dearth in *Dear Brutus* shortly afterwards — Will, who had lost his imaginary daughter in the wood — so unbearable to me, at ten years old.

Life was not all air raids and drama. There was the new experience of day school, Miss Tullock's of Oak Hill Park, which Angela and I attended for a year to eighteen months. I enjoyed every minute of it. Angela, who was much more conscientious over her lessons, was not so sure. Miss Webb, of the third form, was a dragon, and scored through her sums with a blue pencil, so that D, upset by the tears Angela shed over her homework, would ring up his business manager Tom

Vaughan and say, "Tom, old man, these damn decimals, I can't do them for her, can you?" What's more, Tom Vaughan obliged.

Miss Druce, in form two, was more kindly disposed, and the only time I got into trouble was when I forged M's signature on the weekly report we had to take home every Friday and take back to school again signed by one of our parents. The reason I did so was that M happened to be out at the time and I thought I could save myself trouble.

"Daphne," said Miss Druce on the Monday morning, showing me the sprawling, almost illegible Muriel du Maurier in the red notebook, "did your mother write this?"

"Oh, no," I replied, "I did."

"Don't you realise, dear, that this is very dishonest, and is called forging? People can be put into prison for doing this."

"Oh? I didn't know."

The proverbial water off a duck's back passed over me. But I didn't attempt it again. Besides, with memories of John

Poynton and his power over his fellows, I had gathered a small band about me who obeyed me as leader. We did not bully but our word was law, and a tiresome girl with long curls and yellow shoes dared not protest when I threatened that if she displeased us she might be burnt at the stake. Yes, I enjoyed Miss Tullock's. . . .

"Daphne," announced Miss Druce after a short-story competition in the class, "has written the best story but . . ." she paused, "with the worst handwriting and the worst spelling." So I did not really score. Somebody called Olive got top marks.

Air raids, chicken pox, measles, the threat that all the children might have to wear school uniform, cut short Angela's and my careers at Oak Hill Park, and a nursery governess was for a time our tutor, at the same time laboriously coaching Jeanne, who was slow to read. Not that this mattered, for by now Harrison Ainsworth was in full swing, and she could become whatever character I chose for her. But it must have been in the autumn of 1917, after the air raids had driven us to Cookham, that M was invited by a friend of hers, Mrs. Fitzwilliam, to bring the three of us for a visit to Milton, near Peterborough.

When D heard of the plan he smote his knee with his fist and exclaimed, "It's one of the finest houses in England. You'll never forget it."

"Better than Slyfield?" I asked.

"Slyfield?" His laugh was contemptuous.

We left, one September day, by train for Peterborough. A car met us at the station. We were driven for some time, or so it seemed, when the car passed through lodge gates, standing open, and M said to us, "This is the park." The park? But nothing like Regent's Park with flower beds, a broad walk, and people strolling; these were fields or meadows, surely, with the long drive winding through them, and nobody about.

"Do you mean it's private?" asked Angela.

"Of course," M answered, with quiet pride. "The Fitzwilliam family have lived here for over four hundred years."

This must mean 1500-and-something —
dates were still hazy. I couldn't
remember who was King at that time, but
for a family to go on in the same place
year after year, being born, and getting
married, and dying, never going for a
holiday to the sea, just walking across this
park, was hard to believe. Besides, where
was the house? The drive curved, and
suddenly it was before us, long, grey-
walled, stone, stretching endlessly, great
windows set one upon the other with
crisscross windowpanes, then more stone,
and columns, while to the left the building
turned to form a sort of square, crowned
by a clock tower. Was this it, was this
Milton? In later years, unconsciously and
in dreams, the first impact of the house
upon a ten-year-old child would change,
would fuse with others, but now,
bewildered, startled, the grace and size
were too much to comprehend, and I only
knew that never before had I glimpsed
anything so beautiful, so proud.

The car drew up before a colonnaded
porch. We all got out. Who greeted us at
the entrance I cannot say. Was it the

smiling, white-haired Mrs. Fitzwilliam? And her companion, Miss Watson, with the chow dog Michael? Was it the son of the house, Tom, thirteen years old like Angela, sandy-haired, a little shy? Making friends with them would come later, chattering, having tea, but what absorbed me first, while greetings were exchanged, was the magnificence of the great hall, the high ceiling, the panelled walls, and those portraits hanging upon them, men with lace collars, knee breeches, coloured stockings. Milton . . . Milton . . . I stared about me, absorbing all I saw, and why was it that the child who was usually distant with new acquaintances, disliking encounters with strangers, loath to be invited to other children's homes, felt no sensation of dismay, of being overwhelmed, was instead filled with a feeling of great and instant happiness, almost of recognition, and of love?

The ten days that followed went too swiftly, yet somehow held a lifetime of experience. The big bedroom over the northern entrance that I shared with Angela. The even larger one, facing south, that housed M and Jeanne. Breakfast in the dining room, a butler in attendance, a sideboard set with silver dishes, eggs and bacon, boiled eggs, kippers, even a cold ham, and Mr. Fitzwilliam, round-faced, genial, beaming from the end of the table. His name was George, but I think I am right in saying that Mrs. Fitzwilliam, Evie, called him Billie. Then through the side hall into her sanctum facing south, where she presided, it seemed to me most of the day, over a jigsaw puzzle, inviting offers of help which would turn the confusing and seemingly identical pieces into a final picture. Mr. Fitzwilliam would be next door in his study seeing to his letters. And we children, Tom, a school friend of his, a tutor, and perhaps Miss Watson and the chow, would run out into what I believe were called "the pleasure grounds," and indeed were aptly named, leading to a small lake with a boathouse beside it. Here we could play all morning, all afternoon, or further afield be conducted to the kennels, where the Fitzwilliam hounds, a famous pack, were housed, fed and exercised. Then, possibly the greatest treat of all, a visit to the main portion of Milton itself, which for the duration of the war had been converted into a Red Cross hospital for wounded soldiers.

The pillared hall on the ground floor — not to be confused with the entrance hall, and used, so we were told, as a drawing room in normal times — now formed the living quarters for those wounded men who were convalescent and could move around, either on crutches or in wheeled chairs. There were billiard tables and other games for their amusement. A fine main staircase led to the first floor, and the picture gallery, as it was once, had been turned into wards for the men who were still too ill or too handicapped to leave their beds. Why were we not shy? Why did we sit beside their beds, and joke and talk and play cards with them, Snap or Beggar My Neighbour, and never feel ill at ease? Angela conceived an instant passion for a good-looking young soldier called George. Not to be outdone, McCann was my friend, a canny Scot, who gave us a puff at his Woodbine cigarette when

Matron wasn't looking. So much laughter, so much gaiety, up in the wards there with the wounded men, and the same below, in the pillared hall, and out in the grounds too, where the more mobile would come rabbiting. Once only did I realise how the war must have touched them, and this was when a fresh entry of wounded came by ambulance to the entrance in the great hall.

"Would you like to come and see?" Mrs. Fitzwilliam said to us.

Yes, of course. And we stood there, watching, as the men were borne in on stretchers, bandaged, pale, some of them with their eyes closed, Matron and nurses in attendance. There was little noise. The atmosphere was hushed. Thomas Wentworth, Earl of Strafford, gazed down at them from his portrait on the wall. He had been executed on Tower Hill, Tom told me, in 1641, and now, more than two hundred and fifty years later, watched wounded soldiers arrive from France. Had he lived at Milton too? No, his home had been another house, Wentworth-Woodhouse, but he was a relation, all the same. And past and present seemed to be all one. He was history, in his Van Dyck portrait, and this was history too, the stretchers taking the wounded men upstairs.

That's enough, no more, let's go and play in the unused bachelor wing at the other end of the house, where the beds were covered with dust sheets and made good cover for hide-and-seek. Or help Mrs. Fitzwilliam with her jigsaw that took so long to fit into place, then preen delightedly when she nicknamed the three of us Wendy, Peter and Jim — and I was Peter.

There was another visit to Milton the following spring, but both visits have merged to one in memory. Unforgettable, unforgotten, Milton remains a childhood experience that has never been surpassed for sixty years. It was with astonishment and delight that I discovered, during research of the lives of Anthony and Francis Bacon for my book *Golden Lads,* that their maternal grandmother, married to Sir Anthony Cooke of Gidea Hall, had been Ann Fitzwilliam, daughter of Sir William Fitzwilliam, friend of Cardinal Wolsey, and the first of the family to live at Milton Hall.

There could be no greater contrast between Milton, home of the Fitzwilliams, and 45, Woodstock Avenue, Golders Green, the modest though equally lovable dwelling of my Little Granny, Grandpa Harry Beaumont, and Godmother Aunt Billy. To be invited to stay the weekend with them, on my own without the others, was as great a treat as any I could think up for myself, at the age of nine or ten. It was true there was not much scope for the imagination, and books like *The Tower of London* and *Old St. Paul's* must be set aside for something of lighter weight, perhaps *Little Women,* which actually I found rather harder to understand. But I did not go to Woodstock Avenue to read, I went for the love and delight that radiated from the personality of Little Granny, and the brisk but warmly affectionate attitude of Godmother Billy.

Grandpa, always addressed as Father

by Granny, never Harry, was said to be difficult. I had heard M murmur to D at home, ''Father's being rather troublesome,'' and then, with a quick look at us, *"Pas devant les enfants,"* which I knew meant, ''Not in front of the children.'' This immediately inclined me to be on Grandpa's side — if there was more than one side to take, which, when staying at Woodstock Avenue, I failed to discover. True, he was inclined to be grumpy, though never with me, and would sit in his armchair in the dining room, used as the living room, with a newspaper on his knee, exclaiming now and again against what he called the government, knocking the ash from his pipe against the fender. He would go for his morning stroll wearing a straw hat, a very usual headgear then and known as a boater, but I never knew where he went.

''What did Grandpa do when he was young?'' I asked once, and was told he had been a solicitor, but the firm had failed, and Grandpa had lost all his money. This seemed very sad, and I had visions of Grandpa going for his morning walk and bundles of half-crowns falling out of his pocket and never seen again, which must be the reason why they lived in a small house, with Granny doing the cooking and Billy going every day to be secretary to a Mr. Kindermann who dealt in antiques. It was not until after the war that she became secretary to D instead, and typed all his letters, and had an office of her own at Wyndham's Theatre.

When staying at Woodstock Avenue I shared her room, with a small camp bed placed near to hers, and half the fun of this was to stare at the many pictures and photographs on her bedroom wall, which were nearly all religious, for Billy was High Church and did not let you forget it. A friend had once taken her to see the Passion Play at Oberammergau, an event as tremendous in her life as going to Milton had been for me, and the photographs were mostly of Anton Lang taking the part of Jesus, or Our Lord, as she preferred to call him. Anton Lang blessing people, Anton Lang carrying the Cross, Anton Lang being crucified, and there were also photographs of bishops and priests she admired. On Sundays she and Granny would take me to church at St. Jude's, which was almost as good as going to a matinee at Wyndham's, there was so much to watch, three priests robed in splendour, bowing and bending, intoning, scattering incense. I enjoyed every minute of it.

Saturday mornings were also good. Granny would take me shopping in Golders Green to buy the joint and vegetables for Sunday, and sometimes, later on, rolling her sleeves up to the elbow and wearing her apron, she would make homemade bread that we would eat later, the crisp warm smell of it filling the house. Sunday lunch was quite a ritual. The joint would be borne in by Billy and placed on the table before Grandpa, who carved with great solemnity, and the two vegetable dishes were laid down at the other end of the table in front of Granny. Apple tart, Granny's make again, would follow. And after lunch she and Grandpa would settle themselves on either side of the fire and very soon their heads would nod, and they would both fall asleep. What a waste of time, I used to think, when they had all the night for sleeping, but perhaps when people got old . . . And I would creep out of the window at the end of the room and go into the back garden, flanked on either side by the fences of other people's gardens. Although there was nothing to do there, no one to play with, somehow it did not matter, I was happy, and at peace. Billy would be up in her bedroom writing letters — she had so many friends, she was always writing letters — or she would talk to her pekinese dog Ching which she adored, and which tried to bite her every time she groomed him. Now and again she would look out of the window and wave to me. Somehow it was security, and I did not want to go back to Cannon Hall on Monday morning.

Both Grandpa and Little Granny have been dead now for many years, but lately I found a letter that D wrote to her in January 1927, which may possibly have been when Grandpa died. It runs as follows:

Darling,

Everything in the world that matters to me — I owe to you. If my three daughters grow up nearly as nice women as your and your dear old man's have, I shall not have lived in vain. We all love you very much — you know that, don't you?

Gerald

I can imagine no nicer tribute from a son-in-law, and no matter what the occasion the letter was evidently treasured and put safely away.

Godmother Billy continued to live alone at Golders Green, with successive small dogs, pekes and griffons, until all her family were dead, including my own M and D, to whom she had given a lifetime of devotion, until finally, when she was close on ninety, Angela and I persuaded her to come and live near us in Cornwall in a bungalow at Par, to be cared for by a resident nurse and housekeeper.

She was as cheerful as ever, a small dog on her lap which rejoiced in the name of

Merry, and sitting beside her of a morning, during the last years of her life, I thought how little it had changed, with the same photographs upon her bedroom wall, the small *prie-dieu* by her bed, with candlesticks upon it. Yet instead of Billy spooning me my food, as she had done in my earliest days, tempting me to eat with, "This is for Peter . . . this is for the Redskins . . . this is for the Lost Boys . . ." which never failed to arouse interest and so induce me to swallow, I would be saying to her, "Come on, Billy darling, here's a lovely glass of hot milk. If you don't drink it Merry will."

What had happened? Where had the years gone? We shared confusion.

Once, when good Chris, her nurse, had gone out for the afternoon, the housekeeper telephoned me to say that Miss Beaumont was acting very strangely, could I come? I left instantly, and found Billy leaning on her stick, hobbling up and down.

"Oh, there you are," she said impatiently. "Will you please order me a taxi? I must get home at once."

"Billy," I said gently, "you are home, here."

"No . . . no . . ." She grew more impatient than ever. "I must get home at once to Golders Green. I've left those two little children all alone, and it will be dark in half an hour."

So Time did not exist, for the aged, for the young, and for those of us who sometimes see it open and fold up of a sudden, like a telescope. Were the little children Angela and myself, now both in our mid-sixties, once more dwarfed to our original size in the microcosm of her mind? The housekeeper, Mrs. Husband, watched anxiously from the door.

"Yes," I said, "yes, I see. The only difficulty is, Billy darling, the taxis get so booked, it may take a bit of time, and it's a long drive back to Golders Green."

"Nonsense," she said, "I know it's not far. I've only been here about twenty minutes. I can't think what brought me in the first place."

How right she was, I thought. What brings all of us through the years, from the first cry at birth to the sinking pulse at the end, and whom have we left behind us on the way, what ghosts, what crouching figures by what window?

"I'll ring for a taxi at once," I said, meaning it, quite prepared to have the local car from Par come to the door and bundle Billy and myself into it, not to drive the two hundred and fifty-odd miles to London but instead round and round Par itself until, perhaps, by immense deception, I might persuade her that the bungalow had been transformed into her onetime well-loved home. But the children? Who could enact the children? Invention faltered. The only practical solution was for Mrs. Husband to telephone the people who lived next door to the house where Nurse Chris had gone, in the desperate hope that she might be there. An eternity passed. Billy became more and more angry, would not listen when I explained that the first taxi had broken down and I had sent for another. My trouble was that I identified too easily, I could so see her point. I exclaimed with her at the inefficiency of taxis, and began myself to worry about the children left on their own at the house in Golders Green, small faces pressed against the windowpane. Perhaps we should drive to London after all. At last, long last, Chris arrived. In a moment all was calm.

"It's all right, Billy," she said, "I've telephoned your neighbours in Golders Green, and the children have been taken home. They are quite all right now. And you can stay here with me and have some tea."

"Thank goodness," exclaimed Billy, "now I needn't worry any more. And I should love a cup of tea."

Oh, for the training and instant invention of an S.R.N.! Plus the sedative that she slipped into Billy's mouth with the cup of tea, which would have been brushed from my hand had I dared to proffer it. Nevertheless, Time remained the mystery, and who could ever prove that Billy had not looked back into some Fourth Dimension and seen what had happened once, or what might-have-happened, just as my paternal grandpapa, George du Maurier, had "dreamt true" at fifty-six and written *Peter Ibbetson?* Who can ever affirm, or deny, that the houses which have sheltered us as children, or as adults, and our predecessors too, do not have embedded in their walls, one with the dust and cobwebs, one with the overlay of fresh wallpaper and paint, the imprint of what-has-been, the suffering, the joy? We are all ghosts of yesterday, and the phantom of tomorrow awaits us alike in sunshine or in shadow, dimly perceived at times, never entirely lost.

Adolescence

Adolescence, states the Concise Oxford Dictionary, is growing up; the period between childhood and manhood (from fourteen to twenty-five) or womanhood (from twelve to twenty-one). Being concise, it says nothing of the bewilderment, the surprise, the all too frequent increase in distance between parent and child when the latter stands uneasily on the threshold. Do fathers sense a rival in their son, and mothers a daughter who may supplant them? Old-fashioned reticence was wrong, suggesting shame, even disgust at what comes naturally, but in the last half of the twentieth century, when the Pill is being advised for little girls of fourteen, the age of consent lowered, sex instruction given in schools with diagrams on the blackboard, and what has been called "sex play" between children openly encouraged, it would seem that the proverbial pendulum has swung in a curious direction.

It was, and still is, I maintain, always easier for boys. Puberty comes more slowly, the body's needs somehow satisfied by the body's growth, and at fourteen a trial of strength and prowess between companions is nothing to be ashamed of, is, indeed, a matter for mutual congratulation. It is very different for girls. Even today, the sudden onslaught of menstruation to a child of eleven or twelve can come as a profound shock, and in 1920, when it came to me, all such subjects were taboo, never to be mentioned except in a hushed voice behind closed doors, the victim, understanding imperfectly, left to face uncertainty alone. So, for the mother of the 1970s who is still shy, in our enlightened age, and has an imaginative daughter equally naïve, let what follows be a warning on how not to prepare her for what must follow. Amusing, perhaps, in retrospect, not at the time.

One day, when I was twelve and a half, M called me into her morning room at Cannon Hall and told me to shut the door. She was sitting in her armchair, knitting.

"Daphne darling," she said gravely, "I want to speak to you."

"Yes?"

Already my heart thumped. It must be serious, when she had that voice. What had I done wrong? Had I broken something, or been rude to someone?

"Now that you are twelve," she went on, "you mustn't be surprised if something not very nice happens to you in a few weeks. You have had backaches recently, and this may be a sign."

"I haven't a backache now," I said quickly, momentarily relieved.

"No, perhaps not. But what I have to tell you is this. All girls, once they have turned twelve, begin to bleed for a few days every month. It can't be stopped. It's just something that happens. And it goes on happening every month, until they are middle-aged, and then it stops."

I stared at her, dazed. To bleed, all my life, until I was old? Was it the same as the illness the poor little Tsarevitch Alexis had before he was murdered in a cellar with his parents and sisters?

She must have seen the expression on my face, for she continued, "It's all right, it's not an illness, and it's not even like a cut. It doesn't hurt. But you can have tummyache or backache. I myself have had headaches at the time."

I remembered now. M often had headaches, and was generally rather cross when she had them.

"Does Angela bleed?" I asked, still unbelieving.

"Yes, but I have told her never to talk to you about it, and you must promise me not to tell Jeanne."

Perhaps this was the reason Angela so often did not want to join in our games. She must have been bleeding at the time. Poor Angela . . .

"Now, run along, darling, and don't say anything about this to anyone. You will soon know when it happens to you."

I was dismissed. I left the morning room, closing the door behind me. Perhaps it would never happen. Perhaps I would yet turn into a boy. Lucky things, they only bled when they cut themselves or if they were like the Tsarevitch.

I soon forgot the whole business. In at one ear and out of the other, they used to say. And there was plenty to do, now that Miss Waddell, nicknamed Tod, came every day to give us lessons, and jolly interesting lessons too, history being the best, encouraging Angela and me to take sides. Angela was Lancastrian, I was Yorkist, Angela was a Cavalier, I was a Roundhead, and for prep after tea when Tod went back to her lodgings, which she called "digs," we would have to "Write an account of the Execution of Charles I," which, with his portrait in the hall, was fun to do. Even if my bad writing and spelling kept her awake at night, which she told me it did, this never seemed to matter, and she wasn't cross. And after prep, depending upon what I was reading at the time, whether *Nicholas Nickleby* or *Mr. Midshipman Easy,* the nursery —

now called the schoolroom — could be turned into Dotheboys Hall or the deck of a ship, with Jeanne, now eight, a willing victim.

One morning, when I had raced round the garden after breakfast, before lessons, and was feeling rather tired, the maid who shared our bedroom with us, Alice, came to me with a solemn face and called me up to the night nursery.

"It's come," she said gloomily.

"What's come?" I asked.

"What your mother told you about, some weeks ago," she answered, and picking up my pyjamas from my bed, where I had thrown them, she showed me a curious stain. "Come with me," she said, in a voice of doom, "and I will fit you up with something to wear. Tell no one what has happened."

Yet everyone knew. Tod looked at me with sympathy when I walked stiffly into the schoolroom. Angela stared. M wore her *"pas devant les enfants"* expression at lunch. Only Jeanne, my constant companion and buddy, was her usual self. But deception, never practised before on

82

her, must begin. Why, I asked myself, why? And must this continue, forever and ever? And M had been right. My back ached. I also felt sick. Nothing would ever be the same again. I no longer wanted to run around the garden, to kick a football, to play cricket. It was like having a temperature, it was like having "flu." So what was I to do? I felt the corners of my mouth turn down.

"I don't feel very well," I faltered.

"I think you had better go to bed," said M firmly, "with a nice hot-water bottle."

If this was what growing up meant, I wanted no part of it. Kindness and understanding from adults was no consolation. Jeanne's look of surprise round the bedroom door was a hit below the belt.

"Are you starting a cold?" she asked.

"Yes," I lied.

So it began. The deceit, the subterfuges, of the grownup world, destroying forevermore the age of innocence.

It was all over in four days. Shame and revulsion put aside until the next time. It was not easy, though, to adapt to a new status, half child, half growing girl, nor could I share Angela's appreciation of adults, their ways, their conversation, which must have helped her own progress through adolescence, for she was never without an idol, to reverence, to adore, whether it was one of D's theatre friends who came to lunch on Sunday or the bishop who prepared her for confirmation. Jeanne had her own chum now, Nan Greenwood, of the same age, who came to share our lessons, and although she was never a cause for jealousy and was soon roped in for whatever game I had lined up for them both — whether cricket on the lawn or fighting battles for the Huguenots in the lower garden — I relied chiefly upon myself and the books I was reading for inner solace, when the need arose.

A diary, the first of a long succession, was given to me for Christmas 1920, and the entry for New Year's Day might have been written by a child of five. Here was no budding woman, ripe for sex instruction, but someone who perhaps had been left behind on the Never Never Island in *Peter Pan*.

I quote: "New Year's Day. I oversleep myself. We go for a long walk in the morning and stay indoors in the afternoon. It is my teddy bear's birthday. I give a party for her. Angela is very annoying. Jeanne and I box, and then I pretend I am a midshipman hunting slaves. Daddy says I have a stoop. I begin to read a book called *With Allenby in Palestine*."

The teddy bear and Allenby surely made strange bed companions, but that Allenby was approved of is evident from the entry under "Books Read," at the top of the January list, which states, "Very good." Others follow in close sequence, amongst them *Bleak House* ("Excelent"), *Robinson Crusoe* ("Excelent"), *The Mill on the Floss* ("Soulful"). Yes, perhaps it takes a little while to appreciate George Eliot.

On Wednesday, January 7th, the mood changes. The midshipman's dirk is temporarily laid aside.

"We give a dance. It is from 7 until 11.

We have great fun. There are lovely refreshments. I only have to dance with two girls, all the rest I dance with boys. Marcus Stedall is very nice. I believe he is gone on me.'' This festive mood continues throughout the week, at other people's dances, but alas, the excitement and late hours must have proved a strain, and on the seventeenth, a Saturday, comes the weary entry, ''I am ill.'' And on the Monday, ''I have a temperature of 104 Point 4. We have a trained Nurse to look after us, 'cos Angela is ill too.''

Influenza must have claimed its victims, and the arrival of the ''trained Nurse'' suggests that D and M, invariably at panic stations when any of us had a cold in the head, felt they could not rely on the attentions of Alice, the children's maid. It was hardly surprising that after the temperature of 104.4° the diary went missing, and did not turn up again until mid-March, when, sad to relate, I was out of action again with a sore thumb. Dear Dr. Playfair, who had brought Jeanne into the world, and who must have spent three quarters of his working life motoring backwards and forwards to Cumberland Terrace and Cannon Hall to restore confidence to our anxious parents, had pronounced, according to the diary entry, that, "My thumb is bad because I bite my nails. He also says I am not to do lessons until next term. Huzza! Instead, I shall read Browning with Tod." Which was a lot better than arithmetic and French verbs, and, what was more, without any prep the imagination could be given full scope, as shown by the entry the following day. "Another beautiful day. I play in the garden all day. I pretend I am captured by savages, escape in a boat, and capture a fort. I dig a trench too, and make a dug-out from wire. Nan and Jeanne are going to play too. I read also. My thumb is nearly well." Blessings upon Dr. Playfair, who must have known more about me than I knew myself, and perhaps understood that a bitten thumb suggested some inner tension which was better relieved by playing at savages in the garden in the fresh air than sitting moodily indoors with poultices and a bandage.

Nor was reading Browning's *Pippa Passes* with Tod the only verse to come my way, for scattered here and there in the 1920 diary, without any explanation but evidently scribbled down at white heat after reading, I find:

> Alack, there lies more peril in thyne
>   eyes
> Than twenty of their swords. Look
>   thou but sweet,
> And I'll be proof against their
>   enmity.

Preceded by,

> If I should die, think only this of me:
> That there's some corner of a foreign
>   field
> That is forever England.

Nothing in the diary extracts alongside suggests any connection with Shakespeare and Rupert Brooke. They are all routine. "Went for a walk on Spaniards Road. Quite nice. Play billiards after prep." But in November I find an entry on a Saturday afternoon as follows, "It is a beastly foggy day. I go for a walk by myself down the town. In the afternoon I begin writing a book, it is called *The Alternative*. It is fun writing it."

The Alternative, like *John, in the Wood of the World,* leaves a total blank in memory. Possibly, like many a work of genius, it never got beyond the first page! But "I read also" has a piece of pink blotting paper alongside, and the quotation upon it was not from *The Last Days of Pompeii,* my book at bedtime that November, but lines from *The Princess,* with Tennyson at his most nostalgic.

> Dear as remembered kisses after
>   death,
> And sweet as those by hopeless
>   fancy feigned
> On lips that are for others; deep as
>   love,
> Deep as first love, and wild with all
>   regret;
> O Death in Life, the days that are
>   no more.

The truth was, perhaps, that the state of adolescence was catching up on me, for upon an earlier piece of pink blotting paper there is the drawing of a heart, pierced by an arrow, and the words, "I love Basil," scribbled upon it. This, I know very well, refers to the actor Basil Rathbone, who had performed as the hero in the adaptation of Grandpapa's novel *Peter Ibbetson,* staged some months before. It was time, I must have told myself, that I too found an idol or "crush," as Tod described them, to put up in opposition to the many produced by Angela; and Basil Rathbone, dark and handsome, made a fine candidate, especially when he helped us at the hoopla stall, over which M presided at the annual Theatrical Garden Party. Passion withered when he appeared — I think at a garden party D and M gave at Cannon Hall — wearing a straw boater, and though I tried hard to flog the dying embers (Angela: "You haven't gone off him *already?*") I didn't succeed. I wondered what I should have said had I known that over twenty years later he would act the part of wicked Lord Rockingham in the film adaptation of one of my novels, *Frenchman's Creek,* and in pursuit of the heroine, Dona, crash down a staircase to his death? Possibly *The Alternative,* had it ever been written, might have given him a finer role.

It was no use, though. Kisses "by hopeless fancy feigned on lips that are for others" were not really in my line, not at thirteen. It was far more satisfactory to invent a splendid new character for myself, namely one Eric Avon, captain of cricket in School House, Rugby, and his two chums David and Dick Dampier, to be played by Jeanne and Nan. This game absorbed me until I was past fifteen. It could be dropped and taken up at will, forgotten during family holidays, whether to Birchington, to Dieppe, to Thurlestone or to Algiers, then picked up again as the mood of the moment served.

There were no psychological depths to Eric Avon. He just shone at everything. His moment of triumph came every summer when he played in the annual Rugby v. Marlborough match, and the Dampier brothers could be persuaded to play for Marlborough. Although David Dampier (Jeanne) was a fine bowler, and Dick (Nan) fielded well, Rugby invariably won. No cheating. And then, to the applause of the crowd — Tod and Angela would sometimes condescend to clap — Eric Avon, captain of cricket, would mount to the balcony outside the drawing room, overlooking the lawn, and cap in hand (a pale blue beret) bow to the spectators. Later, imaginary fireworks would explode into the sky, and at bedtime there would be a feast in the dorm — extra biscuits, and fruit, smuggled upstairs. Hoopla with Basil Rathbone could not possibly compete.

The last match was played in July 1922, two and a half months after my fifteenth birthday, when Rugby, as usual, won after an exciting match. The inter-house matches followed, and on July 28th came the grand finale, known as Parents' Day. There was a cricket match, and prize-giving, with Eric Avon receiving four prizes, but for what subjects my diary does not state. The Dampier brothers then performed *Hamlet*, with Eric Avon as spectator.

But it was a sad moment for the captain of cricket. I realised that Eric must now be nearly eighteen, and that this would be his final day at school. He was to go up to Cambridge in the autumn. So it meant good-bye to Rugby. I remember vividly, as if it were today, that while the Dampier brothers cleared the schoolroom after the performance of *Hamlet* (which was excellent) Eric Avon went downstairs and into the garden, and stared out at the cricket lawn, scene of so many triumphs. Then he descended to the lower garden, out of sight of the house, and said good-bye to the many friends who had gathered there. Nobody, of course. Only the May tree, and the herbaceous border. But they represented, that July early evening, all the companions in School House, Rugby, and their parents too. He wept. The moment of sadness was intolerable. Then someone from the house called, "Daphne!" and it was all over. Eric Avon had left Rugby School forever.

I often wonder how he got on at Cambridge, and what became of him. How did he fare in later life? I never knew his background, or where he lived. Was he a gentleman of leisure, sporting an old school tie, watching cricket on a village green? Or did he die young? Nobody ever took his place. And the Dampier brothers faded with him. He undoubtedly owed much to *Tom Brown's Schooldays,* to watching the annual Eton v. Harrow match at Lord's, and to other school stories such as *The Fifth Form at St. Dominic's* and *Teddy Lester's Schooldays,* which were my usual teatime reading before settling to the current novel — Dickens, Thackeray or Scott, surprisingly laced at times by Galsworthy and Maugham.

Yet why did I pick on Eric Avon as an alter ego and not an imaginary Peggy Avon, for *The Youngest Girl in the Fifth* and other novels by Angela Brazil were also teatime reading, and equally enjoyed? Whatever the reason, he remained in my unconscious, to emerge in later years — though in quite a different guise — as the narrator of the five novels I was to write, at long intervals, in the first person singular, masculine gender, *I'll Never Be Young Again, My Cousin Rachel, The Scapegoat, The Flight of the Falcon, The House on the Strand.* None of these characters resembled the popular schoolboy hero, Eric Avon; instead, their personalities can be said to be undeveloped, inadequate, sharing a characteristic that had never been Eric's, who had dominated his Dampier brother friends. For each of my five narrators depended, for reassurance, on a male friend older than himself. Dick, in *I'll Never Be Young Again,* was lost when his friend Jake drowned at sea. Philip, in *My Cousin Rachel,* never really recovered from the death of his cousin Ambrose, who had been his guardian. John, in *The Scapegoat,* gained confidence only when he acted as double for Jean de Gué. Beo, the Italian courier in *The Flight of the Falcon,* played shadow to his elder brother Aldo. While Richard, in *The House on the Strand,* was obedient to the instructions of his scientist friend and mentor Magnus, and was thus transported into the fourteenth century.

The female narrators — and these have been three in number — depended upon no one but themselves: Honor Harris in *The King's General* and Sophie Duval in *The Glass-Blowers* were determined women, and knew what they wanted. The only timid one of the trio was the nameless heroine in *Rebecca,* and she found strength of purpose when she discovered that her husband Maxim truly loved her, and had never cared for his first wife Rebecca.

So if there was an Eric Avon struggling to escape from my feminine unconscious through the years, he certainly succeeded in the imagination, however different from his prototype, for I would identify with my series of inadequate narrators, plunge into their escapades with relish and excitement, then banish them from memory until the next one emerged! Perhaps my father Gerald felt the same urge when he acted Bulldog Drummond, Raffles and Hubert Ware; acting, after all, was in my blood.

The disappearance of Eric Avon from my world may have been partly practical, in that a quarter of the lower garden had been levelled and turned into a hard tennis court, and that same summer the cricket pitch on the lawn above had croquet hoops upon its rolled surface instead of cricket stumps. Both games might have seemed tame to the captain of cricket, but not to us. We were all growing up. Angela went off to finishing school in Paris. Dear Tod had been lured from us by an offer from Constantinople to teach English to the daughters of the Sultan, and Dora Vigo had taken her place, less easy to hoodwink over unfinished prep, with lessons themselves more demanding and exams at the end of every term. But the volumes from the morning-room shelves downstairs were as good for browsing as for learning — Edmund Gosse's *English Literature* and Haldane McFall's history of painting — while D, suddenly interested in our progress, produced for our enlightenment some forty small books on the Old Masters, fully illustrated, and to test our knowledge would open them at random, thrusting a reproduction of a Virgin and Child before us and saying, "Who by?" He was delighted when we got the answer right — Botticelli — Murillo — Perugino — Fra Angelico — and, what was more, quoted the city of origin!

Sunday lunches with the dining-room table filled were no longer the tiresome ordeal they had been once. Conversation with adults could be fun, and both D and M encouraged it. Holidays abroad were memorable experiences, not only for new scenery glimpsed but for new contacts, new encounters, so that the pink blotting paper of the yearly diary became more scribbled upon than ever, with quotations from varied sources apparently bearing no connection with whatever had taken place on the day of entry.

> Fire that heats and does not burn,
> And wind that blows the heart to
>   flame

is followed by the cynical remark, "The fruit that Eve ate was really an orange, and Man has been slipping on the peel ever since."

No idols to notch up beside Angela's long list except for the adored Gladys (Cooper) and her young son John, who since I was twelve years old had been my favourite people outside the family. Indeed, with frequently shared holidays I looked upon both *as* family, and loved them equally. The Lonsdale sisters, our exact contemporaries, daughters of D's great friend the dramatist Freddie Lonsdale, were also amongst my favoured few. Frankie — Frances Donaldson today — and I shared many of the same tastes. We told each other that one day we would write, and properly, not just scraps of stories to be left unfinished, and one Christmas at Birchington we collaborated on a play we called *The Sacrifice*.

We were both about thirteen at the time. The management of the Bungalow Hotel built us a stage, the other guests were invited to watch — amongst them those veterans of the real theatre, Sir Squire and Lady Bancroft — and the Lonsdale and Du Maurier children performed, with one or two others who were also spending Christmas at the hotel. Angela, as a nun, was the star turn. Frankie and I as joint dramatists gave ourselves more modest parts. The plot escapes me, but everyone was slaughtered upon the stage save one survivor, who, as the curtain fell — or, rather, was drawn — declaimed, "And I alone am left to bury the dead!" Afterwards Lady Bancroft beckoned Angela aside and told her she would coach her as Lady Macbeth. This was praise indeed. But neither Freddie Lonsdale nor D gave Frankie or myself any hints on dramatic construction, which was rather remiss of them. Had they known that, after their deaths, we should be the first daughters to write their fathers' biographies, they might have suggested some sort of consultation.

Thirteen . . . fourteen . . . fifteen . . . with Eric Avon still the alter ego, and what have been called "the facts of life" as yet unguessed at and uninteresting.

So how was it that on a summer holiday at Thurlestone, in the midst of paddling and shrimping, aged fourteen just, I glanced up one day to see my thirty-six-year-old cousin Geoffrey, who had divorced his first wife and was staying with us in company with his second, whom he had lately married, look across the beach at me and smile? My heart missed a beat. I smiled back. But why? Where was the difference? I had known Cousin Geoffrey all my life, he was fun, he was amusing, D and he were the greatest of friends and companions, for there were only twelve years between them. So why, why, that particular smile?

I knew, instinctively, that we shared a secret. The smile was ours. As the August holiday progressed so did the understanding, and this was something that must not be told to others. He would wave to me from the golf course, a special wave that D did not see, and after lunch, when we all lay out on the lawn like corpses to catch the sun, rugs over our knees, Geoffrey would come and lie beside me, and feel for my hand under the rug and hold it. Nothing, in a life of seventy years, has ever surpassed that first awakening of an instinct within myself. The touch of that hand on mine. And the instinctive knowledge that nobody must know.

"I think Daph is old enough to come and dance at the Links Hotel," he said one evening, and we all went, Angela, Jeanne, Geoffrey's wife, possibly not M, and as the hit tune of the day, "Whispering," filled the dance room Geoffrey smiled again and held out his arms. Margaret Kennedy's *The Constant Nymph* had not yet been written, but this was it. And I another Tessa. Never any more than this. The dancing, from time to time, and the holding of hands under the rug. No whispers. No kisses. No fumblings in the dark.

The holiday came to an end, and the morning he left he said, "Come and have a last look at the sea." I followed him. We did not speak. Then suddenly he turned to me. "I'm going to miss you terribly, Daph," he said. I nodded. Then he looked up at the cliff above, and we saw D staring down at us. "There's Uncle Gerald, spying," he laughed. "We'd better go." By midmorning he had left, catching the train to London, and all the diary tells me on Monday, August 29th, is, "It is a lovely day. Geoffrey goes. I feel terribly depressed. We bathe and play tennis. I read also."

Which book? Was it Stevenson's *The Wrecker?* Was it *Dr. Jekyll and Mr. Hyde,* both listed around this time? And what urged me to scribble on the pink blotting paper, "He who conquers his own spirit is greater than a taker of cities"? Nothing could ever be quite the same again. I had become aware, through my own experience and not by observing others, or by watching actors and actresses upon the stage, that a glance, a smile, a touch, could bring warmth and a sort of magic between two persons of the opposite sex which they had not known before; and if, for the lighthearted though genuinely endearing twice-married cousin of thirty-six, it had been fun to awaken the dormant emotion of a fourteen-year-old girl, the effect on both of us was enduring. No kisses. No hint of the sexual impulse he undoubtedly felt and indeed admitted, when, years later and myself adult, we talked and laughed about that summer with a true cousinly affection which remained constant until the end of his life — he was even best man at my wedding; but instead, on my part at least, a reaching out for a relationship that was curiously akin to what I felt for D, but which stirred me more, and was also exciting because I felt it to be wrong.

In retrospect, how sensible he was to leave me ignorant, guessing, perhaps, at the naïveté within. So much so, in truth, that when I did eventually hear "the facts" of life at eighteen from a school friend, I stared in astonishment and disbelief. Was *that* what all the love stories I had read had been about? What an extraordinary thing for people to want to do!

Back in September 1921, after the Thurlestone holiday, Geoffrey was given a part in the current success at Wyndham's, *Bulldog Drummond,* in preparation for a tour of the U.S.A. D may have stared suspiciously at his nephew and his daughter from the heights of a Devon cliff, but he was ever generous to friends and relatives in need of a job. But I am not so sure about the American tour. Was it a move to get Geoffrey out of the country? I have never known or asked. But on October 18th the diary reads, "Geoffrey sails for America. We see him off. Oh, I am terribly miserable. When shall I see him again?" And, on the pink blotting paper opposite, the quotation from Browning's *Parting at Morning* was surely, perhaps for the first time, in keeping with the mood within:

> Round the cape of a sudden came
>   the sea,
> And the sun looked over the
>   mountain's rim:
> And straight was a path of gold
>   for him,
> And the need of a world of men
>   for me.

If this was first love, and I believe it was, it found its way into no novel of after years, though writers are said to draw upon their own experiences. Some perhaps; not all. Men and women who have never lived make finer captives on the printed page, or if they have lived, and are historical, then the very knowledge that they belong to a past we have not known ourselves induces fancy. Was this how they thought, and lived, and sometimes lied? And the fictitious hero and heroine — unsuitable description today when few are heroic — are they figments of a dream, are they might-have-beens, like the daughter in Barrie's *Dear Brutus?* Psychologists may have the answer, not the writer. Instincts suppressed may travel to the mind's surface, along with every poem, play and novel read through childhood and beyond. We are none of us isolated in time, but are part of what we were once, and of what we are yet to become, so that these varied personalities merge and become one in creative thought, wearing, at times, an additional disguise, the face and voice of someone observed at a distance and believed forgotten, or bearing the casual gesture of a friend. Every character conceived, and fondly considered by its author to be original, was first seeded in his or her being by means unknown, dating back perhaps through months or years, of doubtful parentage; and just as we ourselves carry the blue eyes of one forebear and the quick temper of another, so the genes of a fictitious man or woman develop as they must and without control.

The child destined to be a writer is vulnerable to every wind that blows. Now warm, now chill, next joyous, then despairing, the essence of his nature is to escape the atmosphere about him, no matter how stable, even loving. No ties, no binding chains, save those he forges for himself. Or so he thinks. But escape can be delusion, and what he is running from is not the enclosing world and its inhabitants, but his own inadequate self that fears to meet the demands which life makes upon it. Therefore create. Act God. Fashion men and women as Prometheus fashioned them from clay, and, by doing this, work out the unconscious strife within and be reconciled. While in others, imbued with a desire to mould, to instruct, to spread a message that will inspire the reader and so change his world, though the motive may be humane and even noble — many great works have done just this — the source is the same dissatisfaction, a yearning to escape.

None of the foregoing would have been understood by the child of fourteen who had spent a few weeks of summer holiday in Devon. Kinship between cousins may have left an indelible mark, and loneliness lingered for a while, though cheerfulness soon broke into the daily routine, with riding on the heath, Jeanne and I spurring the hired horses to a gallop, racing each other on bicycles down to the Vale of Health where Nan lived, going to the Gilbert and Sullivan operas on Saturday afternoons, and then when summer came cricket once more, and for a brief span the adopting of that undemanding alter ego, Eric Avon. Significant, perhaps, that it was this summer that he and I parted, and forever, each going our separate ways.

But "I read also" intensified, then and during the following year, with a lot of Scott, a lot of Thackeray, and R. L.

Stevenson never far away. *Beyond* by Galsworthy was pronounced wonderful, while Ethel M. Dell's *Charles Rex* is described as soppy tosh. I have an uneasy feeling that it was Geoffrey, in a letter from America, who had recommended E.M.D.

In 1923 the pace quickens. Samuel Johnson's *Rasselas* is wonderful, the plays of Sheridan very amusing, *The Picture of Dorian Gray* quite marvellous. Strange that my first encounter with the Brontë sisters produced no more than "charming" for *Jane Eyre* and "very good" for *Wuthering Heights*. Sloane's *Life of Napoleon Bonaparte* in four volumes kept me going for several weeks, and for a time I wondered whether he might take the place of Eric Avon, but either this was too exhausting or the others wouldn't play, so the idea was dropped, and I contented myself with carving the initials N.B. on my desk as a reminder. "Books read" averaged nine a month, which was fair going when lessons filled the mornings, games or walks the afternoon, with prep between tea and supper, and "I read also" snatched in between, at bedtime or weekends.

The pink blotting paper and the quotations disappeared with the advent of 1923, for the page-a-day of the new diary was without them; instead I contented myself with narrating, not only the daily events, but what I chose to call "my thoughts and impressions." These, unfortunately, do not amount to very much, the daily events still taking prior place, at any rate during holidays, with paper chases over the heath with myself as hare, scattering confetti, and the Dampier brothers in hot pursuit. And after this tremendous exercise I find, "At lunch had a nasty misunderstanding with M, which rather spoilt the day, but later it came all well." What could it have been about, I wonder?

Poor darling M, was I a trial to her? Never ill mannered, never rude, of that I am sure, but perhaps I made some unfortunate remark that caught her in an off mood. She was not an easy person to understand, and both as a child and as a growing adolescent I could never feel quite sure of her, sensing some sort of disapproval in her attitude towards me. Could it be that, totally unconscious of the fact, she resented the ever growing bond and affection between D and myself? He was her whole life, and next to D came Jeanne, petted and adored though never spoilt, while Angela and I — until we were both adult and life adjusted itself in the way it does — came off second best.

The tensions of family life can never be fully understood by parent or by child. Both crave for love, on their own terms, and give either too much or too little. The possessive mother, demanding, searching, possibly does more damage to daughter or son than the indifferent one, her thoughts elsewhere; nevertheless in both cases seeds are sown of doubt, of insecurity, and the child who cannot rush to his or her mother in moments of stress, telling all, will look elsewhere for comfort, or become a loner.

So, after the awkward lunch, "Spent the evening writing my book," but what the book was remains a mystery, though "A long letter from Tod to cheer me up, explaining life a bit, and saying my book sounds like Compton Mackenzie's *Sinister St.,* which I haven't read" suggests it may have been a story I began around this time about a small boy called Maurice, who certainly wasn't Eric Avon.

Tod, returned from Constantinople, was a splendid correspondent, and frequently came up to Cannon Hall to see us, her visits always a joy. Her recommendations for my readings, however, were somewhat strict, and in her next letter she warned me on no account to read Volume II of *Sinister Street,* which was *"pas pour les jeunes filles."* I promptly got hold of both — they were downstairs in the morning room — and enjoyed them equally, though the matter undesirable for *jeunes filles* passed over my head.

Dora Vigo continued to teach Jeanne, Nan and myself, but Angela, who had been "finished" at Mademoiselle Ozanne's in Paris, was now, to use the current idiom of the twenties, officially "out." Though never a debutante in the strictest sense, she went to grown-up dances, met young men, had a mass of friends, and had acquired a certain status in our younger eyes, particularly as she was given an "allowance" and could buy her own clothes, while we still had Saturday pocket money for sweets.

Wireless entered our lives. A set with headphones was installed in what had been called the billiard room, and an entry in the diary states, "I listen in to Marconi House. The head-receiver much clearer than the gramophone, and we can hear opera, which is marvellous."

Both Jeanne and Angela were far more musical than I was. Angela had her voice "trained" and Jeanne already played the piano very well indeed, and showed promise at drawing and painting. My only talent seemed to be writing stories, which Dora Vigo, with some perception, suggested I should do instead of essays, and during the lesson period. An entry says, "D reads some of my short stories. Seems to think they are good. And Billy [now his secretary] is going to type them." Then the following day, "I tell Miss Vigo about D liking my stories. She admits that she always thought them good but said very little at the time. I am glad."

The novel about the boy Maurice seems to have been abandoned, nor do I know what the short stories were about, although vaguely there is an impression of one that I called "Fog," about a man and a woman leaning over the Thames embankment, who had loved each other once, and now met and talked without recognition. The last sentence ran, "The fog suddenly lifted." Books read give little indication of the source of inspiration. It could hardly have been H. G. Wells's *Country of the Blind,* but you never know. . . . Thoughts and impressions are scattered here and there in the diary pages. I had been promoted to dinner in the dining room, before D went to the theatre, and remarks dropped *en passant* led to reflection.

"I've been thinking. At least, conversation at dinner led to the thought, how cruel it is for people to be averse to anyone with a tarnished reputation. Men don't mind having what they call a good time with girls 'like that', but they are so beastly condescending about them because of it. I think it's snobbish."

Or, "It's funny, when one is out in a street, or walking on the heath, how interesting people one doesn't know can be. One can make everything in life jolly if one is interested."

But another day, apropos of heaven knows what, "I suddenly thought how awful just being married would be. I should be so afraid, so terribly afraid, but of what? I don't know. Oh, I do wonder what my life will be. I can't see ahead. Only death, perhaps, which might mean so little."

Then, in the midst of a carefree Easter holiday in the New Forest — just we three sisters on our own, although our parents had taken care to see that staying in the same hotel was not only Dr. Playfair, his wife and son, but the loved nanny we had first had at Cumberland Terrace, now in charge of another brood — the diary entries filled with walks in the forest, pretending to be Robin Hood while Jeanne was Little John, comes the reflection,

"There is a married couple here, so happy with one another. Yet it makes me feel lonely. I don't understand. There's a longing somewhere." On the following day, "After lunch my happy couple leave. It's extraordinary how they've affected me. Both nothing-out-of-the-way, and yet, I don't know. I shall never be able to love like that, openly and calmly. Then Jeanne and I take tea out in the Forest and read."

The book was *The Forsyte Saga,* and in three weeks' time I should be sixteen. . . .

The summer holidays that year of 1923 were spent at Little Holland Hall, near Frinton, and Christmas at Monte Carlo followed by Cannes. Interest in the adult world about me gathered momentum. Golf, tennis tournaments — the Wimbledon stars were there in force, and we got to know them — dancing in the evening, gala dinners, a "crush" on an older man who was D's contemporary; I even had my bitten nails manicured for the first time in my life. Eric Avon, Napoleon Bonaparte and Robin Hood seemed a world away.

But after the gala dinner and waltzing round the room with the fifty-year-old on New Year's Eve, the diary ends on a sombre note. "What have I achieved this year? Nothing." Followed by a rush of lyricism.

Come, let us seek what we have never
   sought before,
Namely, Love and Beauty on a
   Sylvan shore.
Do you remember how we sought
   together
 The wind-tossed shore in wintery
   weather?
And the cowslips kissed the bees,
And the elm-trees mocked the
   breeze,
And the sea-gulls ruled the seas in
   summer weather.

The tide of adolescence was running at full spate not only then but during the succeeding year. Thoughts and impressions are occasionally conveyed in unintelligible French and Italian, which Dora Vigo, shortly to be married and to become Mrs. Mead, was endeavouring to drum into me before setting up house with her husband in Fitzjohn's Avenue. After this I would walk down to her every morning for tuition, while Jeanne and Nan would continue to share lessons at home with a new governess. This innovation was promotion for me, and I enjoyed it. Nevertheless, "The old discontent creeps upon me for a while. Vague longings forever unfulfilled," and a desire to get away to the country as we had done to the New Forest the year before. "There would be primroses there, and violets hidden under moss, and perhaps a stray bluebell by a pool. And wood-pigeons building in a fir-tree, and robins everywhere. Why doesn't someone write an ode to a blackbird? To think that Byron died a hundred years ago today. . . ." No Byron quote, surprisingly, but a stray thought from Oscar Wilde instead: "Artists make the world a mirror for their moods."

Wilde filled many reading hours that year, winning the highest marks, but a more lasting impression was made by the stories of Katherine Mansfield, introduced to me by Tod, who had a brother in New Zealand, and I felt instinctively that if I could only one day in the distant future write some sketch that might compare, however humbly, to hers, then I need not despair. We never knew, until much later, that Katherine Mansfield and her husband John Middleton Murry were living at that time not five minutes away from Cannon Hall, on the edge of the heath. Curiously, the light from one of their back windows was always shining when I threw ours open in the bedroom, still called the night nursery, that I shared with Jeanne, and I used to wave to it every evening before climbing into bed. Coincidence? A strange one nevertheless.

Meanwhile, a photograph of Michelangelo's statue of David became my pinup, and I tried to draw him as he might look in the present day, without much success. When and if, I told myself, I should ever marry, my husband must look like this. (An impossible ideal, but the reality was not so far out, eight years later!)

A sketch of a man being hanged brought a macabre note into the current diary, inspired by a visit to Pentonville Prison with D, who was rehearsing a play called *Not in Our Stars,* concerning murder.

Major Blake, the Governor, showed us everything. Echoing corridors, locked cells, prisoners abed in the hospital, and finally the condemned cell itself, and the short walk across a passage to the hanging-shed. He even demonstrated how the drop worked. Finally, the graves outside, Crippen, Bywaters and others. A unique experience for two impressionable girls, Jeanne and myself, and deeply imprinted on the memory, the cell, and the drop, sketched on the diary page. But then, D as a father was also unique, and if he wished to see what a condemned prisoner is forced to see, then so could we, and let imagination do the rest. I have wondered since whether the Governor was shocked. Whether the following gloomy lines were inspired by the experience I cannot say.

Sorrow for the men that mourn,
Sorrow for the days that dawn,
Sorrow for all things born
Into this world of sorrow.
And all my life, as far as I can see,
All that I hope, or ever hope to be,
Is merely driftwood on a lonely sea.

Perhaps they were an expression of sympathy for Dora, Mrs. Mead, who told me that autumn, with some shy reserve, that she was expecting a baby in March and lessons must cease. A baby? Oh well, married people usually had them. But it meant a change of routine, and plans were soon under way for me to go to finishing school in Paris, as Angela had done, though to a different one, and in the company of a friend known from childhood days in Regent's Park, one Doodie Millar, who had been to boarding school in England and knew their ways.

How would it be, leaving home for the first time? Should I be homesick? Should I get on with the other girls? Time would tell. I didn't care. The excitement this Christmas was that darling Gladys was once more to act Peter Pan, and that Angela had been chosen by Uncle Jim (J. M. Barrie) to act Wendy. Not that I envied her. To appear before an audience on the stage would have been agony, even in a play like *Peter Pan* which we both of us knew by heart, but at least she would see Gladys every day, and D would produce her to make sure that all went well. Which indeed it did. "The first performance," states the diary on December 18th. "Angela very good. Lots of people, and all like her." And the next day, proudly, "Angela had very good notices."

But for myself, on New Year's Eve, "Oh God, another year wasted. . . . I shall remember, one day, how wonderful it all was."

Paris

Fifty years ago it was the "in" thing, for parents who could afford it, to send their daughters to Paris to finish their education. Not so, I understand, today; Switzerland is the country of choice, and even more expensive. So, with purse strings tight, English girls are in a minority.

Angela had been moderately happy, though homesick, *chez* Mademoiselle Ozanne, and I doubt if I should have been "finished" at all, but for Dora Mead's expected baby putting a stop to morning lessons in Fitzjohn's Avenue. The finishing school chosen was outside Paris, at Camposena, near Meudon, surrounded by an extensive garden or *parc;* doubtless it was considered that this would be healthier for Doodie Millar and myself than being in Paris itself. And if I was unhappy or homesick I could leave at the end of the term.

To the surprise of the family, and of myself, I was neither. Indeed, the novelty of being plunged into the atmosphere of boarding school, the set routine of classes, frequent excursions into Paris by train, new faces, new sights and the delicious sense of humour of my childhood companion Doodie — we shared a room, and were allowed a gramophone and a fire to warm the icy room (an extra, I suspect, asked for by M because "Daphne has a delicate chest") — made the experience one of intense excitement, increasingly so as the weeks progressed.

First, however, came a blow to pride. There were four classes. In the *première* were the elite, those who were academically bright and proficient in French. Next came *deuxième A,* for the able but not brilliant. Then *deuxième B,* somewhat inferior. And lastly the *troisième,* for the duds, unlikely to progress further. I was mortified to find that Doodie and I, after a brief test, were placed in *deuxième B*. After Tod's and Dora Mead's tuition, I had seen myself with the élite! At least we were not in the *troisième,* which was some comfort, nevertheless . . .

I cast an envious eye at the élite, who took it upon themselves to descend from the *galerie,* where we all assembled, to the dining room before the rest of us, so that they were able to choose their places at the various tables, either beside the boss and owner of the establishment, a middle-aged Englishwoman with white hair called Miss Wicksteed, known as "Wick" ("a decent jolly old thing," says the diary), or, more stimulating, beside the *directrice,* Mademoiselle Yvon, thirtyish, slanting green eyes, and a manner that seemed a blend of sarcasm and veiled amusement. She was said to have her favourites, and the chosen few would follow her, after supper, to a room called the *salon du fond,* where they would play a game known as Truths — the more fainthearted would emerge in tears

125

— while the rest of us lesser fry would dance with one another in the *galerie,* foolishly, giggling, or else listen, yawning slightly, while Miss Wicksteed read aloud.

I set myself a goal. Even if I were not in the *première* I would — by hook or by crook — get myself somehow to the *salon du fond.* My roommate Doodie, despite the fact that she knew two members of the élite at home, the daughters of Sir Patrick Hastings, K.C., had no such ambition; she was perfectly content to dance in the *galerie* or chatter with the amiable crowd of the *deuxième A* or even the *troisième.* So one evening, with studied nonchalance, and without invitation, I strolled into the *salon du fond,* a book under my arm, *La Femme au Dix-Huitième Siècle,* and settled myself down to read.

The group by the fireplace stared. Astonishment was evident, even hostility. Conversation ceased. Then Mademoiselle Yvon, a glint of laughter behind her eyes, motioned me forward. *"Venez près du feu, mon enfant,"* she said. And I knew myself accepted, even welcomed. The élite could do nothing. My triumph was complete. Even Eric Avon, bowing to the crowd from his balcony above Lord's cricket ground, had never achieved such a victory.

The trouble was that this time I had entered the lists against live persons, not imaginary beings, and just as Cousin Geoffrey had awakened dawning emotion in a naïve child of fourteen, so the flash of interest and the amused tolerance that I dared perceive on the part of the *directrice* created, in the equally naïve schoolgirl of eighteen, what I felt must be undying passion.

Lessons became of small account, lectures passed me by, visits to the opera, to the Louvre, to concerts were unheeded unless they could be enjoyed in the company of Mademoiselle Yvon, while a place on her left or right at the dining-room table made all the difference to my day-by-day. My excessive devotion made little impression on anyone but myself. "Everyone at school has crushes," said my roommate Doodie. "I think I'm getting a crush on Mademoiselle

Vincent," and she instantly placed herself beside this beaming little red-haired teacher when opportunity occurred.

This was all very well. I knew everything there was to be known about crushes. Angela was never without one on somebody, male or female, and enjoyed herself enormously throughout. This was surely different. A smile from Mademoiselle Yvon and I was in heaven. To be ignored, when she was obviously preoccupied, was hell. Once she dropped a handkerchief in the *galerie* and I seized it, unperceived. Then, on an expedition to Paris, I bought a bottle of scent and anointed the handkerchief; and later, in the *salon du fond,* presented it to her with all the gallantry of Sir Walter Raleigh spreading his cloak in the mud before Queen Elizabeth. The smile, and the inevitable glint of amusement in those green eyes, kept me going for days. Less harmful, maybe, but as insidious as a drug to an adolescent of the 1970s, the approval of my idol became necessity. I was well and truly hooked.

And Mademoiselle Yvon herself? Here

is the dilemma. It seems unkind, even disloyal, to impute mixed motives to someone who became the most devoted of friends, the wisest of counsellors, an unfailing correspondent through months and years until her death from leukemia in middle age, and who gave the same devotion and good counsel to my own daughter when she too became eighteen and studied French under Mademoiselle Yvon's care in her own home. In 1925 none of this could be foreseen.

Nor can I flatter myself that my appearance, my intelligence, or any originality then possessed was superior to the rest of the élite who followed in her wake to the *salon du fond*. I suspect now, half a century later, that at thirty, unmarried, the only child of parents living in Normandy, the prospect of the next ten years as *directrice* of somebody else's establishment was hardly encouraging; she hoped for wider interests and greater financial security. Therefore the background of the favoured few in the *salon du fond,* and of these ex-pupils who still came to visit her, was of importance.

Who were their fathers? Had they standing? Were they eminent in the professional, business or artistic world? If so, they might be useful. *On ne sait jamais*. And with Gallic logic, combined with a genuine love and understanding of the puzzled and often bewildered adolescents who jockeyed for position in her shadow, it was perhaps not altogether surprising that, having heard via Miss Wicksteed of my origins, the daughter of the foremost actor-manager on the London stage, the head of his profession, who knew everybody, she soon raised me to the proud position of first favourite.

So instead of staying one term I stayed three, and dependence upon my idol was such that I turned down, without a qualm, the chance of a holiday with the family in Italy — to the astonishment and surely chagrin of M and D — and was even permitted, at the end of July, to accept the invitation of Mademoiselle Yvon to accompany her to La Bourboule in the Puy de Dôme, where she was going — it was a health resort — to take a "cure."

In retrospect, the invitation, and even

more the acceptance of it, seems amazing. Nevertheless, I went. My cup of happiness was overflowing. The diary, full of ecstatic praise, makes tedious reading to my sceptical middle-aged eye; more interesting by far is the intensive "I read also," the reading invariably in French. Maupassant and more Maupassant — strange contrast to the Katherine Mansfield of a year ago — Anatole France, Paul Bourget, Jean Richepin — and instead of quotes from English poems, the more cryptic French.

> *Quand on sait plaire,*
> *Surtout à la cour,*
> *Que peut-on faire,*
> *Et nuit et jour,*
> *Sans un peu d'amour?*

Reading and writing home to the family would occupy my morning, while Fernande — it was Christian names by now — went for her treatment, whatever it was, I was never quite sure, and then after lunch we would take the funicular up to Charlannes, the beauty spot set amidst pines in the hills above La Bourboule, have tea and, according to the diary, "read, or talk."

I cannot believe I said very much myself. Like most Frenchwomen Fernande was a great *raconteuse,* and once launched upon a theme scarcely drew breath — her stories richly embellished with touches of her own (which I took for gospel truth), interposed, here and there, with an ironic shrug of the shoulder. Her own past sounded, to my eager ears, highly dramatic. A fiancé Marvel, killed in the war, leaving her heartbroken. A cousin in Normandy who wished to marry her, but for whom she felt no passion in return. A close friend, a film star on the French screen, killed instantly in a motor crash, the shock of hearing this profound. Fathers of ex-pupils who had made certain suggestions to her, their wives absent. A banker in Paris, always willing to assist financially, if . . .

How much of it was true? I shall never know. At eighteen, all this was grist to me, I questioned nothing. Here was an adult, whom I adored, treating me as confidante. And when letters came from Paris over which she frowned, or if at lunch or the evening meal her mood, instead of being one of gaiety and humour, should turn to narrowed eyes, silence, a tap-tapping of fingernails upon a plate, an impatient glance over the shoulder at other guests at other tables, my heart would sink, and I would ask anxiously, *"Qu'y-a-t-il?"* only to receive the devastating reply, *"Je m'énerve."*

Je m'énerve . . . Words, impossible to translate, epitomising the total unpredictability of feminine psychology, leaving the bewildered witness wondering whether she was personally at fault. Somewhere, buried in the unconscious of the eighteen-year-old, must have been the embryo writer observing, watching, herself unmoved, noting the changing moods of a woman dissatisfied with her mode of life and temporarily bored by her young companion. The seed of an idea, sorting itself from others, might take some five and twenty years or more to germinate and come to the surface, fusing with later observations, these observations in their turn blending with characters from long-forgotten books, but finally a story or a novel would emerge, and neither the model nor the writer, by this time mature, would be aware of the transformation or of its origins.

After the holiday at La Bourboule I was home again for a brief spell, and apparently already starting on some short stories, for the diary says, "Billy brings me a typewriter from the theatre, so that I can type out my stories." But later the mechanics of changing the ribbon proved beyond me, the stories flagged, and despite riding, tennis and frequent outings to see plays and films the pages have a plaintive note, temporarily lifted by delight at the success of *The Last of Mrs. Cheyney,* the play by Freddie Lonsdale in which D and the loved Gladys were acting together.

The last term at Camposena, to which I looked forward with longing, because it meant not only reunion with Fernande but also promotion to the *première,* proved in the long run somewhat disastrous. I caught flu, the flu went to my chest, a leading Paris physician apparently found a spot on my lung (I was not told about this at the time), and the family at home became extremely anxious, as I was rapidly losing weight. An American friend of theirs, Mrs. Gilbert Miller, living at the Crillon Hotel in Paris, stepped into the breach and suggested I should at once be removed from school, stay with her at the Crillon, and go for "treatment" every day to her own doctor, said to work wonders.

Reluctant, sobbing, I was forcibly removed from my bed and taken by car to the hotel, feeling no longer a confident member of the *première* but more like a child of three snatched from a foster mother's care. The luxury of the Crillon was no consolation, the steam-heated room overpowering after the cold at Camposena and the kindness and flow of chatter from Mrs. Gilbert Miller something I could willingly have done without.

"Could Mademoiselle Yvon come and see me?"

"Yes, dear, of course."

But the visits were snatched, very naturally, leaving me tearful, and as for the daily treatment of the Swiss doctor (a quack of the first order), this consisted of injections of sal volatile, ampoules of salt solution, the laying of electric pads upon my stomach and exposure to violet rays. This treatment was, so an attendant informed me, highly successful with middle-aged ladies, but this was the first experiment with anyone of eighteen. Small wonder, perhaps, that I soon weighed less than seven stone, and I had letters from the family suggesting that a holiday in Switzerland after Christmas might be the answer. My spirits rose. Could Fernande take me? But wouldn't it be fearfully expensive? Then, hypochondriac, "I've lost another 500 grammes."

The upshot was that in the first week of December M and Jeanne arrived at the Crillon Hotel for consultation with Mrs. Gilbert Miller and the doctor, who not surprisingly advised that a journey to Switzerland was unnecessary, and that it would be far better if I went home for

Christmas and returned to Paris after the New Year and continued with treatment for six weeks. Perhaps the "younger sister" would also benefit? M wavered, but Jeanne immediately caught a heavy cold — it was snowing at the time — and it was evident that injections of sal volatile and electric pads on the stomach were not for her.

More consultations. Fernande, invited for dinner at the Crillon, met M for the first time. Sick with apprehension, I wondered how it would turn out. "Everything goes off successfully," I reported in the diary, "Fernande and M hit it off all right," and it was arranged that I should come back to Paris after Christmas, stay with Fernande in a small hotel near the doctor's clinic and go for my treatment every day. When term started and she must return to her duties at Camposena, then Angela would act as my companion and take her place. But afterwards? What then? "Finished" in every sense, would I be considered "out" like Angela, given an allowance and permitted to spend it as I chose? Or would it mean the old familiar routine, riding on the heath in the morning, walks on the same heath in the afternoon, scribbling poems and stories that remained unfinished, and "I read also" until the end of my days?

"The finish of security," I wrote on New Year's Eve. "Doubt lies ahead. *Adieu les jours heureux.*"

It was my misfortune, both as child and as adolescent, and even at eighteen and a half, having attained a semi-adult status, to wake up in the morning like a pregnant woman feeling sick. Invariably so before a journey or when anything pleasant was likely to happen. It never occurred to me that the reason was nerves from repressed excitement.

Monday, January 4th, 1926, was no exception. I was returning to Paris for my "treatment," and although the thought of the many injections did not worry me I was anxious that the Hotel du Rond Point might not come up to Fernande's expectations, or, worse still, that she might be regretting her promise to look after me. "A strong wind and a dangerous-looking sky, and I feel sick as usual," says the diary, and the fact that Freddie Lonsdale was crossing in the same boat in the company of Lord Beaverbrook, who at once offered me his cabin, appeared to make little impression on me.

"I lie down in Beaverbrook's cabin and am not sick in spite of rough crossing, and he gets some official the other side to wangle me through customs. Long boring journey." Obviously I was not an aspiring journalist or I might have made better use of my time.

The welcome sight of Fernande, waiting behind the barrier at the Gare du Nord, smiling and in a good mood, was all I wanted. I no longer felt sick. And oh, the delight of speeding in a hooting taxi through the streets of Paris, the sights, the sounds, the very smells so different from London, the strolling crowds happier, more lovable, the cafés already filled under the bright lights of the Champs Elysées. The stuffy Hotel Crillon was ignored, and the cheerful, modest —

in 1926 — hotel in the Rue de Ponthieu ready to receive us.

Here, all about me, was the Paris I had only dimly perceived during the past year at school, escorted to the opera, to the Louvre, with a bunch of irritating English girls — the Paris which I knew to be awaiting discovery. And realisation came to me that this was what the grandfather I had never known had loved, this was why he had written *Peter Ibbetson, Trilby, The Martian,* in wave after wave of nostalgia as a middle-aged man dreaming of his boyhood, of his birthplace. Paris was his city. It was now also mine, and would become increasingly so, on each successive visit, but alas, on the present occasion, for a bare month only. The six weeks recommended by the Swiss doctor must be whittled down to three, the expense being formidable, and Fernande had been asked by D and M to break the news to him. Perhaps the fact that during his previous regime I had lost such a lot of weight made it easier for her! I listened, in some embarrassment, to the rapid argument between them, the doctor insisting that he could do nothing in so short a time, while Fernande, all her canny Normandy blood rising to the surface, rubbed finger and thumb in front of his face and declared, *"Mettons que cette enfant n'a pas le sou, voilà,"* which apparently did the trick, and he bowed acknowledgment. Whether he reduced his charges for the three weeks I never discovered. Perhaps they came to "an arrangement."

The lost pounds were soon recovered, not by the injections of sal volatile or salt-solution ampoules, but by daily lunches at a restaurant close by, Le Cheval Pie, where the hors d'oeuvre were as filling as any banquet, and Fernande, canny as usual, chose our table directly in front of the spit where the chickens were roasted, the smell of them whipping the appetite. Better still, there was a slight step in the middle of the restaurant floor, so that the clients, advancing for lunch, invariably tripped and all but fell — some did — immediately in front of us. Weak with laughter, I would eat anything that was put upon my plate, and soon we would have the chef turning the spit, and the *garçon* in attendance, joining in our fun. Even the *maître d'hôtel* hid his smile behind his hand, as he elbowed his discomfited clients up the offending step.

Lunch concluded, a brisk walk along the Champs Elysées, or a taxi to the Bois, or a tram to the Boulevard Montparnasse, and a return stroll along the quais of the *rive gauche,* fingering the books, the air icy cold and clear with more than a hint of snow, but who cared? Why couldn't London be like this? Then back to hot chocolate and brioches and éclairs for tea at the Hotel du Rond Point, visits from Cyril and Maurice Le Bas — amusing young brothers of one of Fernande's ex-pupils, Irène — laughter and talk, followed by reading more Maupassant, Paul Bourget, Pierre Louÿs, sups, and an early bed.

It was over all too soon. Fernande returned to Camposena for the spring term, Angela came out to relieve her for a few days, I had my last treatment, my last lunch at Le Cheval Pie, and we were on our way to the Gare du Nord and the dreaded Channel crossing. *Adieu les jours heureux* . . . "A grey, wet day. A thick white fog. Horrid morning to wake up to after a night full of bad dreams. I wailed in my sleep, according to Jeanne!"

Poor David Dampier had a troublesome companion on her hands for the next few weeks, obliged to listen to my interminable moans on how much I loved Paris, and why could I not live there forever? Yet even on that first day home I set myself a goal. "After writing to Fernande I begin to plan some stories. 'The Old Woman,' 'The Welcome,' 'The Terror.' It's going to be rather a task, I'm afraid. The actual writing and constructing of them all, it's pretty hopeless. In the afternoon, feeling tired and deadly bored, I go for a walk across the heath. A heavy sky and a queer hidden sun. Oh, God!"

In retrospect, what patience and tact were shown by D and M — especially M, who could so easily have been brusque and disapproving — towards their unexpectedly moody second child, usually the first to laugh and join in any fun. How about going to a matinée at the Hippodrome? Yes (grudgingly), if you like. And what about the first night of Ivor Novello's new play *The Firebrand?* H'm . . . yes. Then a real bait to lift the discontent. M suggested that I should learn to drive her little car. The Calcott. Allen the chauffeur would teach me. Was it her own idea or D's? I shall never know. Enthusiasm was awakened. The clouds dispersed. "I get on jolly well," was my first report, followed in a few days by, "I drive through London, and all over the place. In parks, along tram-lines, everywhere. Oh, I do enjoy it."

No instructors in those days, no tests by an examiner before the handing out of a licence; merely keep to the left, and bang on the brakes when necessary. Even a skid into a passing car did not deter me, though it must have dented the Calcott. By the end of February I was picking M up from her hairdresser's in London and thinking nothing of it. But self-pity still simmered beneath the surface. "Everyone at dinner says how well I am looking. If only they knew what I felt like inside they'd talk differently. I guess I hide my feelings pretty well, if I want to. They don't know my mind is starving." And this despite the "I read also" of Claude Farrère, Zola and Maeterlinck.

"Daph, darling, would you like a dog of your own?"

A dog? Yes, I would. The truth was that I had never really forgiven M for having given away my West Highland Jock when we moved to Cannon Hall. He had been replaced by a mongrel fox terrier Brutus, a great character, whose love of football exceeded even his love for me, so that when walking on the heath and spying a game in progress between two teams, not of children but of men, he would dash into the forward line, seize the football between his teeth, and bear it off across the heath in triumph. Then, after visiting the vet in Hampstead High Street for a minor complaint, he transferred his affection from me to him, leaving home every day to sit upon the vet's doorstep, until the embarrassed man was obliged to telephone and ask if we minded very much, but he really hadn't the heart to turn the poor dog away. After that, Brutus would call upon me occasionally at home, to see that I still survived, wag his tail and depart once more to the High Street.

Of course I minded. I loved dear Brutus. But I saw his point in preferring the vet and the High Street to day-by-day at Cannon Hall. So the suggestion of another dog was a welcome one, and with memories of my first love, Jock, I chose another West Highlander, and gave him the same name. We fell for each other on sight. He slept in my room, became my shadow, was civil to the resident family pekes, and when I went riding in the mornings would dash upstairs to the top landing, spring on a chair there and watch the window until I returned.

And yet . . . "I go off for my ride as usual. There was a wind that blew about my hair. I'm a harmless, quite decent character when out in the open air like that, on a friendly horse — no people — 'the heavens above, and the road below me.' But it's when I get back into the house, and the same things happen every day, that I go into a kind of silent frenzy, and a mist of hate comes over me for it all. Yet as far as I know I am sane as I write this. Nothing proves that I am mad. Why then these unnatural feelings I can barely hide? I saw a collie dog herding up sheep today in such a marvellous way. How clever they are, these trained dogs. It makes me want to round up sheep on an African farm. What an idle dream!"

I must start to work, I decided. I must get on with those short stories. But "The Terror," about a child's nightmare, seemed so feeble when it was finished, and "The Old Woman," a sketch about a French peasant, equally so. I should never be able to write like Katherine Mansfield. As for getting anything printed . . . No, unrest was more easily expressed in verse, which nobody but myself would ever read.

There was a beacon on a windy hill,
Strangely alone it was, and strangely
    still,
Steady and straight it rose into the sky,
While yawning at sea tired sailors
    wondered why

147

Stars in comparison seemed dim — but
   bright
And steady shone the beacon's light.

Close to the hill there was a path
   that led
Down to a wood that was untenanted
By any flower, or any living thing;
Deep pools there were, thick trees,
   also a ring
Of dark misleading paths, no passer-by
   would care
To wander from his way and trespass
   there.

Then, from beyond the sea, there
   came
An irritating wind, which bore the
   flame
Down from its upward course towards
   the wood,
Where quiet and unprotected the tall
   trees stood.
How eagerly the flame's caressing
   tongue
Licked the dry bark, and how the dark
   wood swung

In joy and deep content at being
   burnt.
The fire dried up the pools, and even
   learnt
The secret of the paths, till there
   were no more
Strange and mangled treasures to
   explore.

Now there are no more leaves, and
   the fair
Trees and ferns are stunted in despair.
All is quite still, and there is no
   sound,
Yet there are ashes spilt upon the
   ground.
The fury of the beacon was too great,
Himself, and the wood, he has
   destroyed, their fate
Was thus predestined by a strange
   desire,
The longing of a forest for a fire.

The poem, scribbled on the diary page
headed "Statistical Summary," intended
for accounts, is undated, but the faded
blue ink in which it was written closely

matches the daily entries for February and March for that year, 1926. What prompted the image? I have no idea. It was not until six months later that M, Angela, Jeanne and I were to spend a brief week in Cornwall, nor on that occasion did we walk to the Gribbin headland. Indeed, nearly twenty years would elapse before I came to sit, day after day, writing in my hut at the end of Menabilly lawn, staring out of the window at that same headland, where a beacon had once stood, and now on its former site the Trinity House landmark was a warning to mariners, the dark woods close beside it. No burning fires. No devastation. Only those that imagination kindled. But the headland was there, and the wood, perceived long ago in some passing flash of thought. Perhaps, for the first time in my life, I had, aged eighteen, a moment of extrasensory perception!

I must have told Jeanne, who was ever sympathetic, about my dreams of rounding up sheep and cattle on a farm, because one day she announced that a friend of hers knew of a farm in Cumberland, near Lake Derwentwater, where they took lodgers, and what fun it would be if we could go for a few weeks in the Easter holidays. Greatly to our delight, M approved of the idea, and decided to book rooms. She would take us, and stay for ten days, but D would never spare her for more than that, and how would it be if I wrote and asked kind Mademoiselle Yvon to come up and join us for the final week? How would it be? Sick with excitement I wrote off at once, but Fernande's first reply was disappointing. She had promised Miss Wicksteed to take a party of girls to Rome. She did not see how she could get out of it. My spirits sank to zero. I had seen myself, not perhaps rounding up sheep, but climbing hills with incredible dexterity, way ahead of Jeanne, then looking back over my shoulder for Fernande's nod of approval. It would be like La Bourboule over again, where admittedly she had spent most afternoons relaxing in a chaise longue on the heights of Charlannes while I roamed about exploring, but then that was because of the "cure," and the cold sharp air of Cumberland would be a cure in itself.

A second letter brought renewed hope. She *might* be able to come for that last week, the dates for Rome were uncertain, but she should be back in sufficient time to take the train to London and so to Cumberland.

So it was settled, and on April 7th M, Jeanne, Jock and I caught the ten thirty-five from Euston to Keswick, arriving at our destination some time after seven o'clock. A kindly Miss Clarke welcomed us at the farm, set high in the hills the other side of Derwentwater, M approved of the rooms, and we sat down to a hot supper in the sitting room, in front of a blazing fire. My only fear was that Jock might misbehave, but he settled at my feet as if it were the nursery at home.

Mountains, woods, valleys, farms — holidays in the south of France, in Algiers, in Dieppe, could not compare with this, my first experience of rugged scenery, of running water coursing through the hills down to the lake, and the names of those hills — Cat Bells, Causey Pike. No skipping up them as I had seen myself, but a steady jog, pausing for breath, and Jock — perhaps his West Highland blood — truly in his element, until one morning he plunged into a fast-running stream, turned on his back and began to drown, and I had to plunge in after him, getting soaked through in the process, M and Jeanne calling out in horror from the bank. Had I but known it, the scene was prophetic. . . .

Walks and excursions filled our time, one of the excursions being to Dove Cottage, Grasmere, where Wordsworth had lived. Seeing his personal things, his desk, just as they had been when he was alive and writing there, impressed me deeply. Yet more than this the lakes themselves, mysterious, often shrouded in mist, and with little islands upon them like the island in *Mary Rose,* I noted in my diary, and the people, our farming family the Clarkes, so honest, so true. ''How different from everyone in London,'' I wrote. ''There is nothing artificial here, no insincerity, no falseness. If their only interest is in farming, then this is real. I love them. I love them all.''

Perhaps I had felt the same emotions before, about the strolling passers-by in the streets of Paris, but somehow this was different. A new awakening. A feeling for the countryside as opposed to a city, a desire for roots in the soil. . . .

Fernande arrived for the last week, replacing M, but alas for any climbing feat up Causey Pike. It rained every day. Even the view from the farmhouse window was blotted out, while Fernande, exhausted from the school tour around Rome, seemed weary and out of sorts, though she made valiant efforts to appear cheerful in front of Jeanne and the farmer's bustling daughter, Miss Clarke. Indeed, I teased her unmercifully one morning when, entering our sitting room, I caught her holding forth, in her fluent English, upon the talented Du Maurier family of French extraction, a grandfather whose books had sold the world over, and a father who was the greatest actor on the London stage. Miss

Clarke, eyes wide, listened in silence. It was obviously the first time she had heard of him. "Doing a Miss Clarke" became a code word forever afterwards between Fernande and myself, and she had the sense of humour to appreciate it.

The last day came. Good-bye to the hills and lake I had grown to love, for all their mist and rain, and the tiring journey back to London.

Poor Fernande. A shock awaited her when she arrived at her small hotel near Russell Square. Expecting to escort the school party back to Paris the following morning, she found a letter from Miss Wicksteed, briefly announcing that her services were no longer required. In short, she had been sacked. No reason given. No word of explanation. What on earth would happen to her now? Bewildered, I saw her into a taxi en route for the Grosvenor Hotel, where Miss Wicksteed was staying, to "have it out," and returned home to Hampstead. Whether M and D expressed sympathy my diary does not say; they were fully occupied with the dress rehearsal for

Edgar Wallace's play *The Ringer,* which D was producing at Wyndham's Theatre, and the first night was to be in two days' time. I spent an anxious night, and hung about most of the morning waiting for a telephone call, while the family went off to the Private View at the Royal Academy. Such smart occasions were not in my line, and certainly not on that particular day.

Finally, the telephone rang. Could I go down to Fernande's hotel at once? I arrived, to find her pacing up and down in great distress. Yes, she had seen Miss Wicksteed, who had given no proper explanation, and had herself left London in charge of the school party that morning. Her job was finished. But why? I asked. Why? Had there been any disagreement the previous term? No, none. Had things gone wrong in Rome? No. Could it possibly be that Miss Wicksteed had disapproved of her coming up to Cumberland to stay with us? No. What she chose to do in her holidays was her own affair. *C'est fini, voilà tout.* She must immediately get in touch with the father of an ex-pupil who had often given her advice and might be able to help. She would see him that very afternoon. And then, for the first time in all the months I had known her, she looked just a little embarrassed, glanced at me uncertainly, and said, "Do you think there would be any chance for me in the theatre?"

"How do you mean?"

"As an actress, on the stage," she replied. "I have sometimes thought I might have some success. After all, Yvonne Arnaud is French, and she has made such a career over here. Should I ask your father, perhaps?"

I felt myself go scarlet. Oh, no. . . . Oh, how awkward. . . . Oh, what could I say? Fernande, without any training, to imagine for one moment . . . and what parts did she hope to play? Her French accent was very strong, it just wouldn't work. I could see D patting her on the shoulder, smiling, saying, "My dear, you would hate the life, I only act because I'd be useless at anything else. You have the talent for understanding the young, which is far more important." I swallowed and said quickly, "No, no, it wouldn't do. Please forget it. D wouldn't be able to do anything for you."

There was silence for a moment. Then she nodded.

"Perhaps you are right."

During lunch we discussed the possibility of her starting up a small finishing school of her own in Paris, with no more than half a dozen girls, perhaps, and the question of an acting career was not mentioned again between us, either then or in after years. Did she truly see herself as a second Yvonne Arnaud, or was it a bow drawn at a venture, just in case? I shall never know. The following day the ex-pupil, daughter of the influential father, and I saw Fernande off from Victoria in the train to Paris, and in the evening I went to the first night of *The Ringer,* a great success, and on to Edgar Wallace's party at the Carlton.

The General Strike was about to begin, but I was more concerned over the future of a Frenchwoman out of a job than with the English miners.

The country might be heading for chaos, no tubes, trains or buses, people walking to work, giving or being given lifts in cars — D enjoyed doing this on his way to the theatre — but Hampstead remained the same, and hearing the first cuckoo with Jock by the Leg o' Mutton pond struck me as being more sensible than listening to reports of the strike on the wireless. Also it was imperative to get down to some writing. I settled myself every day in the loggia above the tennis court and made a start. Very slow going. Every line must tell and somehow come right. How on earth, I asked myself, did Edgar Wallace manage to turn out a book a week? "If only I can stick at it," says the diary, "and eventually make some money."

The point was, I had no intention of living indefinitely on an allowance from the family, intended for dress, tube fares, cinema and other modest expenses. I should be nineteen in less than ten days. I must somehow be more independent than Angela, who was perfectly happy living at home, with masses of friends of all ages; in and out of the theatre world, she was never at a loss for something to do. And Jeanne was equally happy at her Hampstead day school, developing a new prowess in hockey and also making a circle of friends. I did not want any friends. "I would like to go out and live my life in some new colony, where things are just starting, new. Somewhere away from decadence, and modern materialism. Away from Europe. Perhaps South Africa, a farm, where there would be no town life, and plenty of riding. I can see myself in my mind's eye, free. Perhaps Fernande could come out and look after me." Well, of course. Someone who was rounding up cattle and sheep all day could hardly be expected to come back and cook and clean!

"I sit down all afternoon and do more writing. It comes very slowly, though. It's so much easier to think out vaguely in my head than to set it down in words."

I must read more books. M gave me a subscription to the Hampstead Library, and here was a new interest, after taking Jock out for his daily walk, to prowl around the shelves, history, travel, biography, literature. "I can look up everything I want to know, and have the use of any book. Really great fun. I come back with a life of Cesare Borgia." Which hardly seems the most suitable reading for a sheep farmer in South Africa, nor the volumes on insanity and mental disease which followed it. Grist, though, to the apprentice mill.

Twelve pounds in tips for my birthday was now put aside against a future fare to Paris, perhaps in July, and, what was more, I had a brilliant plan of using the interest due on a War Loan investment of £500, which we sisters all possessed, amounting to £95, and offering it to Fernande to help her buy a house and start a school. She refused, to her eternal credit. Nevertheless, the £95 would bolster my own finances if I wanted to travel, for writing stories would probably never get me anywhere.

"I wrote better at fifteen than I do now," I grumbled in the diary, after glancing through some scraps that had not been lost. "Perhaps if I changed from fiction to sociology I should do better. A treatise on civilisation? It might be good practice for style if nothing else.''

The truth was that any excuse served to lay down my pen or much-bitten pencil. Films, plays, the opera, I enjoyed them all, either in Angela's company, or in M's, or with my ex-roommate Doodie, who had taken to dancing and developed a passion for the Russian ballet. Edgar Wallace, his wife Jim and daughter Pat were forever forward with invitations, Ascot amongst them. There was Wimbledon with M, and after the first night of a Noël Coward play we picked up D from the theatre and went on to a ''small, smart party at the Victor Pagets', with a good band, and Jack Smith sang, and I danced with the Prince of Wales! Nice, but rather a pathetic figure. Didn't get home till half-past four.''

This, my only encounter with the future King Edward VIII, seems to have made less impression upon me than a scratch at the front door of Cannon Hall a few days later, after dinner, and who should be there but my old dog Brutus, who had decided to call and enquire after my health?

"He was thrilled to see me, and I let him in and patted him, and we sat together for about half-an-hour. Faithful old chap, he really is an amazing dog. After a while he trotted off again, back to the vet in the High St." I wondered if he had hoped there might have been a game of football?

Or perhaps he guessed I was off abroad again, for in mid-July, with family consent — rather to my surprise, though Godmother Billy made a good ally — I set forth for Paris once more. I spent a night in a somewhat sleazy hotel near the Gare Montparnasse, and the following morning Fernande and I took the train for Brittany. She had booked rooms for her much-needed holiday at Trébeurden, on the coast, a glorious spot, with an almost deserted beach beneath our hotel windows. She was in poor shape, however, exhausted with searching for a small house in the Paris suburbs where she might start her school, for, despite assistance from bank managers, agents and friends, nothing had as yet turned up. Disappointment, and the extreme heat of midsummer, had affected not only her nerves but her heart as well, and I had alarming visions of her suddenly collapsing, hand pressed to her side, and myself not knowing what to do.

In a panic, on the second night of the holiday, I drank too much wine at dinner, had to be helped up to bed, and was violently sick. "My God," I wrote, "I've never felt so ill in my life! I didn't know what was happening. How filthily squalid." Bitter remorse followed, but I had learnt my lesson. Never again would I "indulge" so freely, then or later, and I am pretty confident that Fernande had refilled my glass on purpose that evening so that the lesson should be well and truly learnt.

Prospects for a pleasant holiday brightened. Fernande became less depressed, and I went swimming every day, climbing rocks and going for long walks. Excursions to other places along the coast by char-à-banc were exciting, stimulating. Farms in South Africa were forgotten. I must live by the sea, somewhere on the coast of Brittany, where there would be rocks to climb and pools to comb, and I could bathe naked with nobody by. Perhaps an island would be the thing? There was an island off Trébeurden, the Ile Molène. I used to stare at it with longing, for it was uninhabited. Once we hired a boat with a local fisherman and sailed around it, the white beach untrodden. Yes, an island. But perhaps not Brittany, maybe Greece. I didn't know. . . . But the sea must be close, there had to be the sea. And there was something touching about the little chapel on the cliff above Trébeurden, where the local Bretons burnt candles for their fishermen, where they prayed for their protection against sudden storms.

I began to write a short story called "La Sainte Vierge," only a sketch, but it echoed my mood, and reading was continuous, always in French, with the inevitable Maupassant the favourite choice, laced, rather surprisingly, with D'Annunzio and Voltaire, whose *Candide* I found "marvellous, witty, and ironic." Fernande may have been preoccupied with her own future, but she saw to it that

I did not waste my reading time on trash.

Then, in the midst of all the rock climbing and swimming, she came down to the beach one morning with a sad face.

"I've had a letter from your father," she said. "There's bad news for you."

She explained, gently. Then I read the letter for myself. D, returning home one night from the theatre, found no Jock in his basket. M told him he was nowhere to be found when she had herself gone upstairs to bed. Intuition made D walk down in darkness through the garden. He found Jock, drowned, lying in the rainwater tank below the greenhouse. He must have chased a cat which had sprung into the bushes above, fallen into the tank, which was full of water, and been unable to climb out.

Once again I saw the Cumberland stream, and the little body on its back; this time I had not been there to rescue him. And by a strange, eerie coincidence the old dog, Brutus, had called at home the same day to look for me, and on returning home had been run over and killed.

"They knew. They both knew," I said to Fernande.

"Knew what?" she asked.

"The two dogs. That they would never see me again. It was a sort of sacrifice."

I turned away, unable to explain to her, or to myself, what I meant. Nor, fifty years later, can I explain it now. Only a lover of animals will understand the sudden feeling of loss, of emptiness, and the intuitive bond which exists between man and dog, has always existed from the beginning, and will, please God, continue to the end.

A sympathetic letter came from M the following day, enclosing more money, and suggesting that as the weather was so good we should stay on in Trébeurden for a further three weeks. So it was agreed. And like all sadness, when we are young, the memory was put aside, the shock thrown off, while the remaining days brought new incidents, new sights, new readings of Maupassant to stimulate the mood. Only once, in the diary, did I mention the two dogs again, and this was to express a wish that they had met each

other and become friends. "But where?"
I asked myself. "And how? What happens
to them after death, to us, to everyone?"

When I arrived home at the end of
August everyone told me how well I was
looking, and that it was evident that living
by the sea suited me.

"D and I have been thinking," M said,
"that it would be a good idea if we could
find somewhere, a house of our own,
perhaps in Cornwall, where we could all
go for holidays, instead of abroad. Edgar
has been so generous over *The Ringer*
that we could afford it. You'd like that,
wouldn't you? Lots of swimming, and
walking."

Y . . . es. Was it a family plot, I
wondered, to keep me from whipping over
to France when the mood urged? If so
. . . still, I would wait and see. And
anyway, Fernande hadn't found a house in
Paris yet, so her plans were still
undecided. Meanwhile I must start
writing again, but instead of short stories
I had hit on what I thought was a brilliant
idea for a play in blank verse, blank verse

representing, to me if to nobody else, something in metre that did not rhyme. "Every line must be perfect in its way," I scribbled in the diary, "and it will be difficult to do, but interesting. I've already thought out a very chaste love scene, and the hero is a Greek called Diomedes."

Whether this hero was the fabulous King of Thrace, finally devoured by his own horses, which had been nourished on human flesh, or the King of Argos and a hero of Troy, I have no idea, for, alas for posterity, the blank verse drama seems to have been lost! Encouragement came from Angela, who confessed that while I was in Brittany she and her great friend Betty Hicks had been looking through my desk, and had found the start of a short story called "Lundy" which they both thought very good. There were some poems, too. Why didn't I show them to D? I did, after Sunday supper, and to my genuine surprise he professed himself delighted. He became reminiscent, as always on a Sunday, alone in the dining room, and told me how he had always hoped that one day I should write, not poems, necessarily, but novels. There was plenty of time.

"You remind me so much of Papa," he said, "always have done. Same forehead, same eyes. If only you had known him."

Grandpapa, strolling with his dog on Hampstead Heath. Sitting down to work every day in his studio. I could never be so industrious. How strange. . . . Then I remembered Paris. But of course. That nostalgia for his boyhood days, for Passy, so that forever afterwards he was somehow torn between two countries, and although successful and happy kept dreaming of the past, wondering about those French ancestors he had never known. Yes, I might well be like that one day. But not yet. The present was the thing. And good news came from Fernande: she had succeeded at last in finding a small house at Boulogne-sur-Seine, the other side of the Bois, and if she could gather together a few girls for pupils it would be possible to start the term by the end of September. She had already booked the sister of an ex-pupil from Camposena, and did I know anyone? Yes, I did. Angela, who had been staying in Devon with the Lonsdales, knew that Mab, Freddie's youngest, was hoping to "finish" in Paris. Mab came up to Hampstead to spend the day with me, and was delighted at the prospect. So two pupils booked — this was excellent. And, with luck, I might slip over myself in the autumn to see how it was turning out.

First, though, this business of looking for a holiday home in Cornwall, and the three of us, Angela, myself and Jeanne, with M, left for Looe on September 13th.

"I wasn't terribly keen to go," I wrote in the diary, "because it means no time for my writing. However, I didn't say so, and it will be nice to get some sea air."

The lack of enthusiasm was soon dispelled. We were none of us inspired by Looe, and the following day M hired a car and we drove on to Bodinnick ferry and Fowey harbour. The jottings in the diary are staccato, excited.

"Bang on the river is the most divine little house for sale, which we all go mad about and want at once. M will see the owner tomorrow.''

Brittany forgotten so soon, the Ile Molène and its deserted beach? Fernande's new home off the Bois de Boulogne likewise? Risking repetition I quote, not from the hurried diary, but from some opening passages in a book called *Vanishing Cornwall,* which I was to write some forty years later.

''The hired car deposited our mother and ourselves at the foot of the hill, by the ferry. We could either cross the ferry to Fowey or lunch at the Ferry Inn here in Bodinnick. It was nearly one o'clock, and we chose the latter course. Before climbing the hill to lunch our eyes were caught by a board saying 'For Sale' on the gate just above the ferry. Beyond the gate was a rough piece of ground and a house by the water's edge, a strange looking house, built like a Swiss chalet.

'' 'Yes,' said the ferryman standing near by, 'they call it Swiss Cottage. They used to build boats there, down under, and have the second floor for lofts. The top floor was for living. It's for sale right enough.'

"We went to the inn for lunch and afterwards, during coffee, our mother talked with the proprietor. We were touring Cornwall, she explained, with the idea of looking for a house for the holidays; we came from Hampstead, London.

"I was too impatient to wait for the conversation to drag on. I jerked my head to the others to follow me, leaving my mother talking. We went down the hill. My sisters tried the gate by the ferry and went into the yard. I found another gate, and a pathway leading to the other side of the house. Here there was a garden, or what went for a garden, terraced uphill tier upon tier, and the chalet part of the house thrust itself forward, built, so it seemed, against the rock, with the windows facing straight out across the harbour. I went and stood beneath the chalet, the water immediately below me, and looked towards the harbour mouth. There were small boats everywhere, and yachts at anchor, but more stirring still a big ship was drawing near, with two attendant tugs, to moor a few cables' length from the house itself.

"There was a smell in the air of tar and rope and rusted chain, a smell of tidal water. Down harbour, round the point, was the open sea. Here was the freedom I desired, long sought-for, not yet known. Freedom to write, to walk, to wander, freedom to climb hills, to pull a boat, to be alone. It could not be mere chance that brought us to the ferry, and the bottom of Bodinnick hill, and so to the board upon the gate beyond that said 'For Sale.' I remembered a line from a forgotten book, where a lover looks for the first time upon his chosen one — 'I for this, and this for me.'"

Between Two Worlds

Swiss Cottage was bought and renamed Ferryside, and a team of builders and decorators set to work during the following months to have it ready for occupation by late spring. As M had so rightly said, none of this would have been possible but for *The Ringer* and the generosity of Edgar Wallace in sharing the royalties with D, who had rewritten much of the dialogue. We were all delighted, although D, who liked to think of himself as Cockney born and Cockney bred, had yet to be introduced to harbour life. However, if it turned out anything like Whitby, where so many of his own boyhood holidays had been spent, he told us he would feel perfectly at home.

"Papa was never happier than at Whitby," he said on one of our Sunday strolls across Hampstead Heath. That was true. I had forgotten. Fowey was a port for the shipping of china clay, and had no fishing fleet, yet both towns had harbours; the smell of tar and rope, mingled with sea water, must surely be the same. So here was another bond in common with the grandfather I had never known. Meanwhile, if I was ever to write another *Trilby,* which was extremely doubtful, I must get to work.

I was allowed the use, that winter, of the room over the garage at Cannon Hall, reserved up to now for D's friends who came to lunch on Sundays and wanted to change their clothes before tennis. A curious ritual, when today we wear the same clothes throughout the day, whether eating or playing.

Here, above the garage, was real privacy, but the room had only a skylight, and was dark in consequence. Not very conducive to inspiration. But I was determined to finish the "blank verse" play and write some more poems before starting, or rather finishing, the few short stories already sketched. The reason for this was that my cousin Gerald Millar — brother of Geoffrey — read for Heinemann's the publishers, and, evidently prompted by D, suggested I should lunch with him one day, bringing my poems, and he would see whether they were interested.

So, towards the end of October, I met Gerald at Heinemann's, where he introduced me to "two men of the firm," with whom I left the poems and the play, and we went on to lunch at Simpsons in the Strand. The diary says nothing of my literary hopes, merely that "Gerald is such a dear, and nice to talk to." Possibly Viola Tree, a close family friend, who had herself read the poems, guessed the outcome, for she invited me down to Cambridge, where she was touring in *The Country Wife,* and I had a tremendous time — for Viola was the best of companions — visiting the various colleges, meeting undergraduates, racing at Newmarket, and above all having tea in Jesus College with Sir Arthur Quiller-

Couch, the famous "Q," whose home was in Fowey, and who had heard that the family had bought the old Swiss Cottage. Whether we discussed the writing of poems the diary does not state, but the following morning I had a letter from my cousin Gerald.

"Very nice and encouraging," the diary says, "but they can't publish the poems or play, or do anything about them. I can see that it was rather an ambitious thing to hope for; however, I must do some short stories next."

Undaunted, I went round the Fitzwilliam Museum, and lunched in Trinity College with three charming undergrads, who drove Viola and me to Grantchester afterwards so that we could dream about Rupert Brooke and "Honey still for tea." I returned home elated and full of Cambridge, and immediately went down to the Hampstead Library to borrow 'Q's" *Studies in English Literature*. "I hope we get to know him well when we go to Fowey, but he's probably a very retiring sort of man." Dear Sir Arthur, how he would have chuckled had he seen the entry! Then back to the garage room and my short stories. "Oh dear, I'm afraid people will think them very boring. If they're ever read. This last one all about a poor old man whom nobody loves." It was rather like being in *deuxième B* all over again, with the *première* not merely two terms off but at least two years. One day I would show them. "Them" presumably being the gentlemen from Heinemann's and the reading public.

"I wish I had a dog again — my poor little Jock. . . ." A fortnight later I was the proud owner of a golden retriever pup of seven months, whom I instantly named Phoebus Apollo, Phoebus for short. Like his predecessors he devoted himself to his owner, lying stretched at my feet while I laboured away at the short stories and polished up "Lundy," which had been praised by Angela and Betty Hicks.

Back to kennels, though, for Phoebus, at the end of November, for I had promised myself a quick visit to Paris to see Fernande's new home in Boulogne-sur-Seine. It turned out to be delightfully comfortable and snug, down a side road away from traffic, yet close to the Bois. Her two pupils were happily installed, financial troubles appeared to be settled (exactly how I have no idea), and, best of all, in his own lair beside the house was a rival to Phoebus, an Alsatian called Schüller, the size of a wolf, who, when taken out in the Bois, went for everything on sight, animal or human, unless forcibly restrained by a chain. When he was permitted indoors, no one could rise from a chair without Schüller's permission.

Fernande boasted she could do anything with him, which was true, but reminding her of my first entrance into the *salon du fond* at Camposena I was determined not to be beaten. Within two days Schüller was lying at my feet, a slave! Though walks in the Bois, holding on to his chain, required rather more force on my part.

My fortnight went all too quickly. Staying with Fernande in her own little home was far more satisfactory than being in rooms at a hotel, and, although she had to give up much of her time to the pupils, there was a certain status in being an ex-pupil and a personal friend. I felt superior. Morale was high.

Besides, there was something to look forward to in the New Year ahead. Edgar, not content with his generosity over *The Ringer,* had invited Angela and myself to join his party of family and friends for a winter sports holiday at the Palace Hotel, Caux, in Switzerland. This, something we had never done before, proved a memorable experience, and we enjoyed every moment of it. Edgar was a wonderful host, and Jim, his attractive second wife, considerably younger than himself, was an equally superb hostess, joining in all the fun and teasing her stepchildren, ourselves and the rest of the party unmercifully while positively encouraging us to tease her back.

Skating, luging, skiing — this was more exciting than climbing Causey Pike in Cumberland, and once more I was determined to excel, whether on skates or flat out on a luge down the bob run.

"Of course I can't go fast yet, but people say it's astonishing for my second day," boasts the diary. Probably quite untrue, but the Wallaces, experts all, were ever generous, like their father, and when the exertions of the day were over there were skittles in the bowling alley at the hotel, followed by dinner and dancing. It was new for me, if not for Angela, to be surrounded by youngsters of both sexes bent on having a good time, all friendly at the first introduction, not only those in our own party but everyone else in the hotel; and it never occurred to me that Edgar and D had got together during the autumn and decided that the "loner" of the Du Maurier brood, who had hitherto preferred adult company, and French at that, might be broken into the more rational enjoyment of her own contemporaries by such an experience. It certainly worked, and although I didn't find a young man on whom to have a "crush," as Angela immediately did (not that I was looking for one), the ability to get on with everyone surprised me, broadened my outlook, and made me realise that there was much more "to" the boys and girls of my particular age group than I had hitherto suspected.

Nevertheless, although fun and games was the order of the day, staying up late in the bar and drinking brandy and soda (I boasted of this in a letter to Fernande, who, lacking her usual sense of humour, expressed herself greatly shocked), I still found the conversation of my elders and betters rather more interesting than that of my peers. At nineteen, nearing twenty, I was young enough to enjoy the reminiscences of people older than myself, and Edgar was a delight in this respect, as was his wife Jim. They never "talked down" to me, and, although Edgar was a strict enough father to his own children, the absence of the parental tie between us made talking all the easier.

The trouble at home with D — now that I was becoming adult — was that whenever Angela or I were drawn into a heart-to-heart conversation with him, either walking on the heath, or more usually over his glass of port after Sunday supper, he too easily became emotional, suspicious, even possessive, and this made for reluctance on our part to discuss personal thoughts or our relationships with our friends. M, to her credit, did not pry, though she spoke her mind forcibly when irritated or annoyed, but even now, as in childhood and adolescence, there was little intimacy between us, a mutual reserve.

I think D must have sensed this, for he encouraged his loyalest of friends, Viola, to take me out and about with her on many occasions — the first essay at Cambridge having been successful — and during the spring of 1927 she would suddenly turn up at Cannon Hall and suggest a walk over the heath, or a lunch and a matinée in London, nor did it ever occur to me that the encounter had been organised beforehand. We had another week at Cambridge with the undergrads, as successful as the first, and in March she invited me to join her for a week in Berlin, where she had theatrical affairs to discuss with Rudolf Kommer, business manager for the great producer Max Reinhardt. Work in the room over the garage was progressing slowly, and I was only too glad to accept. Besides, D would pay all expenses, and even in 1927 the

Hotel Adlon in the Unter den Linden must have cost quite something. How would Berlin compare with Paris? I wondered. First impressions were duly recorded in the diary.

"Complete efficiency. Quiet. Few people, little traffic in the streets. Enormous number of people everywhere. Complete luxury at Hotel Adlon, where Viola, excited as a child, turned all the taps on in the bathroom full blast. We dine at a bourgeois café. How the Germans love their food!"

The walk in the Tiergarten the following day was "not as lovely as the Bois du Boulogne," and the people strolling there had "heavy, solid faces." The ex-Kaiser's palace at Potsdam was impressive, however, and so was the palace of Sans Souci, and the *Schloss* in Berlin itself where the ex-Kaiser had also lived, and Frederick the Great. But it wasn't Paris. No, indeed. And a formal lunch with rich people of the name of Schwarber in their grand house made me think longingly of Fernande's little home near the Bois de Boulogne. Insular, no doubt, but during the lunch I kept remembering those air raids of ten years previously, and wondering whether it could ever happen again.

Then, two days before we were due to return home, it was Trébeurden once more. A telegram came from D to say that my golden retriever Phoebus had been run over and killed by a laundry van in East Heath Road. So . . . Another sacrifice. But why? For what reason? Must this always happen to animals I loved? Viola, who adored her own fox terrier Gyp — he had accompanied us to Cambridge — was full of sympathy, but the fun had gone out of our visit, and we returned to London exhausted, after the most appalling sea crossing, Hook of Holland to Harwich, it had ever been my ill luck to experience. The Channel was never like this. Small wonder I wrote in the diary, "I dreamt last night I was a condemned criminal, with only five minutes to live."

Viola, ever resourceful, now introduced me to Mrs. Chase, the chief editress of *Vogue*, with the idea that I might get some sort of job, but exactly what remained very vague. Mrs. Chase explained kindly that there would be no jobs vacant until she found a new London editress; meanwhile, how about writing an article on my visit to Berlin? Oh, dear . . . back to the garage room and more biting of the pencil. What on earth could I say about Berlin? If only I could send Mrs. Chase the beginning of a mournful sonnet.

When at the close of a cold summer's
    day
I gaze into the fire, and hear the rain
Shatter itself against the window-
    pane,
And from without the mournful
    branches stir
Hither and thither with the sobbing
    wind,
When I am startled by the creaking
    floor,
And hear the banging of a distant
    door
Until I have to turn and glance
    behind

To force myself to see there's nothing
   there;
When long-dead visions crowd into
   my brain,
And all alone I live them once again,
When . . .

But Mrs. Chase hadn't asked for a sonnet. Nor had the publishing men at Heinemann's. I wrote my article on Berlin, and I think, though I could not swear on oath, that it was accepted and published. And this was the end of the matter. No staff employment, much to my relief, for this would surely have meant going to an office every morning and being told what to write about. No freedom in that.

A worse fate was suggested some months afterwards. The play of *The Constant Nymph,* a great success in London with Edna Best as Tessa and Noël Coward as Lewis, at which I had wept profusely, was, so it seemed, to be made into a film later in the year, and someone — heaven knows who, perhaps D himself, in an unholy alliance with the future director — suggested that an unknown girl, instead of a trained young actress, might be effective in the part of the Constant Nymph herself. Nobody seems to have asked me for my opinion, and the diary is the only record of the passing whim of the powers in charge.

"Constance Collier rings up, and I've got to go down to a film studio tomorrow to do a test for Tessa in *The Constant Nymph*. I shall feel a fool and it will be very hot-making. Jeanne and I play tennis. I read also." G. K. Chesterton's *The Return of Don Quixote* hardly seems the right preparation for a test as Tessa Sanger. I should have practised facial expressions in front of the bathroom mirror before going to bed.

The following day: "I have my hair done in the morning. Then hang about doing nothing. In the afternoon a car comes for me, and takes me to the studio at Islington. I am led to a dressing-room and am made up, then I have to go down and do my test. Nothing but camera men and the director Basil Dean. Simply awful. I have to try and do a little scene. I

189

was too frightful, I know, and felt such a fool. I was glad when it was all over." I never saw the test, and the suggestion that a great career awaited me as a film star did not come up in conversation after Sunday supper.

Five days later: "Thank God I go down to Fowey tomorrow." I knew now where I wanted to put down roots. And it wasn't Paris after all, despite a happy three weeks at Easter walking Schüller in the Bois, strolling on the *rive gauche,* drinking lemonade through a straw in the cafés in the Boulevard Montparnasse, or reading Balzac while Fernande wrote letters to prospective parents of pupils. It was Cornwall.

Ferryside had been in the hands of the builders and decorators throughout the winter and spring, supervised from time to time by M, who had a great gift for planning a home: she knew exactly what she wanted, and got it. Early in May she went down with Angela to open the house up and see the furniture installed in the proper places, with the willing help of

Viola and of dear Tod, now back again in England after a visit to her sister in Australia. When I arrived with Daisy the housemaid on May 9th it was my first sight of the place since the preceding September, when we had seen the board "For Sale" and knew that this was it.

The transformation was complete. The old storeroom, where boats had been built in former days, was now the living room, with a staircase leading to the floor above. Here, instead of sail lofts, were bedrooms and a bathroom. To my delight Jeanne and I were to share the room that had a door leading into the garden, with a fine view down-harbour; in fact, the very same spot where I had stood the year before and willed possession. The top floor, with the Swiss chalet appearance, would be M's and D's domain, with their bathroom, the dining room and the kitchen.

"The house looks too lovely," reads the diary. "Everything has been done to make it perfect. I am so pleased with it all, and adore the rooms. At high tide we can sit on our quay surrounded by water and

191

watch the sun go down.''

So much to see. So much to do. Never one to flick around with duster or broom inside a house, then or later, I seized a hoe and turned up the soil at the top of the garden — perhaps lettuces could be planted there. But gardening was tedious after a while; so much better to explore, to walk for miles, bluebells everywhere, or cross on the ferry to Fowey, walk through the town, and so to the castle on the cliff above the harbour mouth. The whole excitement being that on May 14th, the day after my twentieth birthday, Angela and M went back to London — Tod and Viola had already left — and I was on my own, for the first time in my life. A Mrs. Coombs came in to cook, but this did not count. I was free, I could come and go as I pleased when I pleased, with no parental or even sisterly eye to watch, to make suggestions.

Why was it, I used to wonder, that being on my own at Hampstead, Angela in London with friends, Jeanne at her day school, plunged me, too often, into a fit of depression? Work in the garage room a toil. Walks on the heath so tame. A general dissatisfaction of mind and body. Yet here in Fowey it was like being someone else. I was never for one moment bored, never depressed. I would awake in the morning and go to the window, and stare out across the harbour. Another ship had come to anchor during the night — what was her name? Where was she from? The water was lapping the slipway beneath the house, and a pilot boat was chugging to the jetties.

Oh, the happiness of those weeks! The thrill of crossing backwards and forwards on the ferry never palled. To stand on the Fowey side, at Passage Slip, and shout "Over!" and after a moment or two to see the cheery wave from the ferry man at Bodinnick, or better still, if a cart had to be transported, to cry "Horse boat!" — none of your car ferries half a century ago. The horse boat, propelled by gigantic sweeps, may have taken double the time its successor does today, but that was half the fun, and if the tide was running strongly there was always the possibility that we might be swept upstream.

No lying in bed here, reluctant to rise and face the day, but quickly up, dressing in old clothes (I must buy myself a fisherman's jersey and sea boots). It was best to potter in Fowey of a morning, when there were no cars, no visitors, only the inhabitants, and the atmosphere was busy, friendly.

D was having a motorboat built — with his customary largesse and total ignorance of local conditions he had ordered it from a shipyard at Hammersmith, London — and I longed for it to arrive. I could hardly wait to go to sea. How would it be in rough weather, though? We ought to have had a sailing lugger, with a deck and a cabin, and I saw myself hauling on ropes, hoisting brown sails, masts creaking — it would be like *The Wreck of the Grosvenor* without Captain Coxon. The biscuits are full of weevils. The pork stinks.

To work, though. I mustn't neglect work. The short story "Lundy" did not satisfy me. It must be gone over, rewritten. And I had suddenly got the idea for another, quite different story, about a smart vicar in London, which would be fun to do and would make D laugh, if he ever read it. Yes, to work, to work. . . . The time flashing by. What, lunch already? Mrs. Coombs would call me "Miss Doreen," and I hadn't the nerve to correct her and tell her my name was Daphne. Then after lunch a long walk, and a furtive trespass to the Isolation Hospital up Pont creek, where so many seamen, I had been told, had died at the end of the war with that fatal Spanish flu.

"They thought they were going there to die," the old crabber told me, "and die they did."

Die they did. . . . I peered in at the windows of the abandoned hut. How grim, how desolate. And those schooners below on the mud flats, also abandoned there to die, their hulks rotting. One with a figurehead at her bows. The *Jane Slade*. What seas had she once travelled? What was her history? And the men who had manned her — all dead, all gone? There were so many stories waiting to be written. Perhaps one day . . .

Then back at Ferryside, high tide on the

slipway, the sun setting over Fowey, and another walk tomorrow, in the opposite direction, upriver, past the jetties. "I walk back by the loveliest lane imaginable, absolutely filled with peace and beauty. I could cry and laugh with happiness. I walk slowly, drinking it in. Tired when I get back, and I read." Kipling's *Captains Courageous,* suitable to the Fowey mood.

But conscience smote me. I hadn't written to Fernande for days, and she would be "on a hard chair," my expression for someone sitting bolt upright while others lounge and chat, forgetting to include the someone in their conversation, originally coined because it had happened to Fernande herself, when visiting me in Margaret Miller's suite at the Hotel Crillon. Oh, Lord . . . and my guilt was the same as when I had forgotten to write to D and M and had received a letter from Godmother Billy ticking me off. "It's rather selfish of you, darling, not to write home and tell them what you are doing, when it's so kind of them to let you be down at Ferryside on your own.''

Yes, of course it was kind, but why must I be reminded of the fact, and would I ever write enough short stories to sell, and so make some money that would be mine, all mine, so that I could pay the cook and buy my own food, and keep myself and be truly independent? It just had to happen. I refused to be beaten.

I finished the story about the vicar, calling it ''And Now to God the Father,'' a splendid title, I decided, suiting my mocking mood. If Godmother Billy ever read it she would have a shock! Then joy, oh joy! What fun! Cousin Geoffrey, Lewis Dodd to my fourteen-year-old Constant Nymph at Thurlestone, whom I had barely seen since, was back in England, staying in Plymouth with his naval brother Guy. Could he come over and spend the day? He could indeed!

I met him at Fowey station, forty-two years old, as gay and debonair as ever, with the same come-hither look in his blue eyes, which now with all the experience of my own twenty years I recognised and accepted for what it was, just himself.

We flung ourselves down on the slipway at Ferryside, not to hold hands under the rug but to talk and laugh, happy and contented, our moods matching. It was like finding a long-lost brother about whom one would always feel more than a little bit incestuous.

"Why can't you stay?"

"I daren't. Brother Guy would be suspicious."

"Come again, then. Soon."

"I will. After Whit Monday."

Which indeed he did, on the Tuesday, and we spent another happy day together, going on one of my tremendous walks. But what amused him most was when I told him that after he had left on the Saturday evening D had telephoned from London, probing, suspicious.

"Has Geoffrey been over to see you?"

"Yes, great fun."

"What did you do?"

"Do? Nothing much. Just lolled about."

My wicked cousin threw back his head and laughed, the most infectious laugh I have ever known.

"Bless his heart," he said. "He's on the

warpath again. We'll pull his leg when you come back to London, and let him imagine the worst."

When I taxed him with being irresponsible he became suddenly serious, and told me he had always been irresponsible, and always would be.

"You know what it is?" he said. "It's our cursed French blood."

I smiled, and thought of Grandpapa working away in his studio, faithful to Granny throughout his thirty years of married life. And Fernande, with her strict Normandy upbringing. French blood my eye, I thought; *qui s'excuse, s'accuse.* . . .

Geoffrey caught the five-thirty train back to Plymouth, and I had no telephone call from D that evening. Nevertheless, a few days later Angela arrived from London. I was glad enough to see her, with her peke Wendy, but independence was at an end, and after a week we were both of us home in Hampstead.

"Wind and tide very strong," I wrote in the diary the day before we left. "I row about in the dinghy but find it difficult to keep her head straight and not drift all the time. Then pack up my few things in the evening. Hate to leave my retreat."

The roots were well and truly planted. It would take more than parental control to dispossess me.

I was back at Ferryside again by the end of July, this time with Jeanne as companion, and, what was more, the gardener Biggins had produced a fat mongrel pup for me, Bingo, half spaniel, half sheepdog, destined to become almost as great a character as Brutus, but with a passion for boats instead of football.

The motorboat *Cora Ann,* named after the heroine in Edgar's play *The Ringer,* was due any day from Hammersmith. The dinghy had already arrived, and despite many a struggle against wind and tide I soon had the hand of her — to hell with wet feet and wetter bottom — while the future skipper of *Cora Ann,* a veteran of Jutland named Adams, became my firm friend instantly.

So many days we should spend together in the months ahead, myself at the wheel of *Cora Ann,* Adams giving directions.

Learning to scull (propelling a boat with an oar over the stern); learning how to steer in a rough sea and not go on the rocks, how to take a hook out of a fish's mouth without squirming, fishing for conger eel up by the jetties after dark, rabbiting when winter came. Dear Adams, the best of companions, tales of Fowey in old days, the pranks he had got up to as a lad; when I asked him about the schooner *Jane Slade* with the figurehead, lying on her back up Pont creek, he was proud to tell me that his wife had been a Miss Slade, and she was the granddaughter of the original Jane.

"There's stacks of old letters in a box," he said, "all about the family, and when the schooner was built. We'll look at them one day."

One day, yes, one day. But first *Cora Ann* had to be unloaded from No. 8 jetty and ready at her mooring for when the family, and more especially D, arrived, D for his first visit to Fowey. And how it rained that weekend! We could not put out to sea, it was far too rough, and there was I all ready to show off my prowess in the boat, not only to D but to Geoffrey too, who came with him before leaving for Canada at the end of the week. All went well, though, despite the weather, and D professed himself charmed with Ferryside and the harbour.

The following weekend brought certain mishaps. M sprained both her ankles and was immobile. Viola, who came down with D, fell into the harbour off the slipway. And D himself, determined to brave rough seas in *Cora Ann,* set forth with Adams and nearly went on the rocks off Polperro through engine failure. He swore Angela, Jeanne and myself to secrecy, and I don't believe M ever discovered the truth. What excuse was made about leaving *Cora Ann* in Polperro the diary does not relate, but next day Adams and I hired bicycles, rode to Polperro and fetched the boat back to Fowey Harbour in "wonderfully smooth seas, catching mackerel on the way." I was glad I hadn't been on board — it might have reflected on my seamanship.

Truth to tell, Fowey was much more fun when both D and M were in London. D because one was always on tenterhooks that if the weather was poor he might be bored, and M because she was — all credit to her — houseproud, and was forever tidying up when sea boots and oilskins were too much in evidence. On our own, Angela, Jeanne and myself, we were never bored and seldom tidy, and life was exhilarating in consequence.

"I've just realised," I wrote in September, "that I think of nothing nowadays but fishing, and ships, and the sea, and a seaman's life. Adams and I go out and catch mackerel until after seven, and after dark we go up to the jetties and I catch a monster conger eel, I'm sure it weighs about 30 lb. It was certainly 5½ feet long." And a few days later, "Off to Polperro in *Cora Ann*. The boat shook and danced in the rollers, and the wind blew into my face, and the sun shone. Glorious feeling. Then we had to go up to the ship *Wearbridge* at the jetties to get ballast, and while Adams is seeing to this I sit in the cabin with the 1st and 2nd mates as they have their tea. I wish they'd take me to Philadelphia as a 'prentice'!"

The following day the *Wearbridge* sailed. "As they passed Ferryside they gave three blasts as farewell, and the officers waved. I went alongside and waved too. Adams said that attractive 1st mate gave the order!"

Oh yes, it was a seaman's life all right, and although I may have fancied myself as Edward Royle alongside the good ship *Grosvenor,* I doubt if the first and second mates looked upon a girl of twenty in quite the same light.

October came all too soon, when Angela and I were due back in Hampstead. "I think Fowey means more to me than anything now. The river, the harbour, the sea. It's much more than love for a person. I don't know how I am going to exist back in London."

And on the day we left, "It's heart-breaking. To go away from this, the one place that I love. Everything is the last act of *The Cherry Orchard.* I go over the whole place before we leave — visit every corner of the garden and gaze for a long while at the sea. I tell them all that I shall be back soon and they understand. It all belongs to me now. One last trip in *Cora Ann* down-harbour before we go. Then the train. . . . Oh God, to exchange this for dreary bloody London. . . ."

At twenty one has little patience. Must I really endure dreary bloody London until Christmas, when we would be Fowey-bound once more? The futility of shopping at Selfridge's instead of going fishing with Adams, arguing across counters, carrying paper parcels, rushing down to the tube in a panic for fear I should be late for a quarter-to-seven dinner before D left for the theatre, and M would frown. "Darling, do try and be on time!" No Bingo to jump into the dinghy — for he had been left behind with Adams — and loll with his head against the gunwale as I pulled down-harbour. The only hope to ring up Mr. Camps at the riding stables and ask if Major, his rather too fresh horse, was free for an hour in the morning. "I show off to myself, and gallop without reins or stirrups, but if I had been at Fowey I might have been out on the whiting grounds, besides a score of other things. The waste of London, I can't get over it." No inspiration, either. An inability to sit down in the garage room and work. Then hard-chair letters from Fernande. "Now your letters are so full of Fowey you won't want to come and stay in Paris again."

Don't say *she* of all people is going to start now? She ought to be pleased that living down at Fowey has made me feel so well, and that it's such a healthy life. In any case, Paris was better than London, although I no longer felt shackled to it as I had done a year ago. "I'm Prometheus Unbound!" says the diary.

November drew near, and I took £35 out of the bank — most of my quarterly allowance — and announced my intention of spending a month at Boulogne-sur-Seine. No family protestations, thank goodness, and to celebrate escape I took D to see the film of *Seventh Heaven,* the current hit of the moment, and, emotional as always, he cried all the way through it. Then packing, and away next morning. The hard chairs were soon softened, Schüller gave me an ecstatic welcome, and the only drawback at Les Chimères (the name of Fernande's house) was the constant presence of Joan, one of the ex-Camposena pupils — before my time — who, for reasons best known to herself, appeared to dislike me. In retrospect I have a feeling she may have lent Fernande the money to buy Les Chimères. And the four resident new girls — for Mab Lonsdale had finished her course — were of *deuxième B* standard, or even *troisième,* so best left to their gramophone and mutual giggles. What it was to feel superior!

A happy month all the same, even with the shackles not entirely removed. The Bois and Schüller glorious in early morning, *"libre, sans chapeau, l'odeur des rues, le marche dans le quartier italien,"* and on the feast of St. Catherine all the midinettes parading on the boulevards, ragging with the students. "I do still feel like one of them, despite Fowey. Well, anyhow, G. du M. belonged here, perhaps when he was my age he felt like this too."

Oh dear, it was hard to be torn between

two places. . . . My cursed French blood! And almost the same day a letter from Geoffrey, returned from Canada, who would be able to join us at Ferryside for Christmas.

Fernande sniffed. "He is a married man twice your age. You shouldn't encourage him."

"But he's such a darling. Such fun. Like a brother."

"A brother? *Je m'en doute!*"

A Gallic shrug of the shoulders, and it was evident she disapproved of cousinly intimacy.

"Well, what about you and your cousin in Normandy?"

"*C'est tout à fait autre chose. Nous sommes du même age!*"

H'm . . . Better keep off the subject, and go with her and the girls to a lecture at the lycée — which they wouldn't understand, silly things. This week the lecturer was to speak on Mallarmé and Rimbaud, and I adored Rimbaud and his *Bâteau Ivre, "J'étais insoucieux de tous les équipages."*

It was sad, though, when I took my last

walk in the Bois with Schüller on December 10th, and waved *au revoir* to Fernande at the Gare du Nord. Life was a series of greetings and farewells, one was always saying good-bye to something, to someone. The choppy seas of the Channel were a symbol of the Styx. . . . My spirits rose at Victoria, though, for Geoffrey was at the station to meet me!

Christmas at Ferryside was a great success, despite the fact that D had not been too well the week before. He must have been going through some sort of personal crisis for, M and Angela having gone to Fowey early, I was left in charge of him, and he kept breaking down and crying. I wondered if he would be well enough to travel on the twenty-first. Luckily Geoffrey and Uncle Coly — widower husband of Aunt May, who had died nearly three years before, and a great dear — came with us, but the journey was something of a nightmare. D recovered at the sight of M and spent the next day resting in bed, so my responsibility was ended; but what a tie married life must be — I hoped it would never be my lot.

All went well over Christmas, no anxieties, no moods, the house gay with holly and mistletoe, everyone pulling crackers, question-and-answer games in the evening, with Geoffrey trying to stroke my knees under the table. Marriage ties evidently did not worry him, although his wife Meg was ill in a nursing home.

His conscience must have nagged him on Boxing Day, for he returned to London, and Ferryside became less lively without him. I stared out across the harbour in something of a sombre mood on New Year's Eve. It was bitterly cold, unusual for Cornwall. We even had snow, but grey and mushy, unlike the glitter of Switzerland last year. How long ago that seemed! Poor old 1927, I felt sorry for the dying year, and composed a sonnet to its memory.

To the Old Year, 1927

It grieves me much to see you desolate,

You who began so well, and in such
    splendour.
So full of blinded hope and high
    endeavour;
That as I watch you pass, and
    meditate
Upon your little failures and the
    way
You shunned responsibilities, my
    heart
Is dumb and heavy that we have to
    part
Before the breaking of another day.
So much you promised that was not
    fulfilled;
Though I beseeched you hover on
    your wing
You fled too fast to heed my
    whispering.
Your feet are weary now, your hopes
    are stilled,
    Faded to dust the dreams you once
      desired,
      Come, let me hold you, for I too
      am tired.

I scribbled "D du M" at the bottom of

the page, shut up the 1927 diary, and opened the clean white page for 1928. . . . What on earth was all that noise? "Suddenly the world went mad. Our world. Fowey harbour. It seemed as if every ship's bell was rung, and every ship's siren blew, and the night, already sufficiently alight with stars and a low quarter-moon, was strung with rockets. It was like the declaration of peace — or war.

"As midnight passed the moon was hidden by a great black crag of a cloud — a bad omen, I wonder? And into my head comes the line 'A year of blood.' 1928. Pray God not. My overheated imagination, startled by those sirens and the clanging of bells. As I went to sleep I knew the morning would be brilliant, and it was!"

Not so brilliant for the rest of the household, however, because before the week was through something went wrong with the kitchen boiler, no hot water, no cooking, fuss and commotion, and everyone decided to go back to London. Everybody, that is to say, except myself.

"I am considered silly, selfish and incredible by all concerned. No use in explaining. I prefer to live happily in discomfort here in beloved Fowey to living comfortably, query, and discontentedly in indifferent Hampstead. That's all. I'm used to being alone. Why fuss? Why struggle? It's funny that no one seems really to understand my craving for solitude, that I am sincerely, and without posing, happiest when alone. It's my natural state.

"There was much last struggle of packing and suitcases, up early, etc, and then they all went across the water and so to the station and London. I was left by myself on the slip, and felt like a child when it builds a sand castle, and stands on the top waving a spade. I can be king of my own little castle for a while. Took my Bingo for a walk up Hall above the harbour, and everything was light and wonderful. The harbour itself a silvered chart, curled grey edges of the sea, lit by mists of ochred sun. I stood there, bathed in a sea of glory, filled with a deep content and peaceful weariness.

213

"J'étais insoucieux de tous les équipages, et comment!"

I started work at once. No garage room as at Cannon Hall, but my own bedroom with a flat desk facing the window and the harbour.

"This is what I've been needing for a long time. There's nothing like it for making the hours fly by — too fast, they beat one's brain and one's pencil every time. I sound like some enthusiastic Kipling — God knows why I've put this in such a hearty way. I worked on my story of 'The Doll.' I like the idea, though it's pretty extravagant and mad. I hope the important bits will come out all right. It's so difficult when I think it over, it sounds weak and hopeless. But it will be a wonderful kick to finish it, probably tomorrow. More power with a story than poem, because there's real sitting-down solid work with it, and a poem for me is more to pass the time, and an exercise for the brain."

This reminded me, when I had finished "The Doll," that I must write a poem about the *Jane Slade,* the schooner with the figurehead lying up Pont creek, which Adams and I had talked about in the autumn. I had made D and Jeanne climb aboard her with me on New Year's Day. Yes, I knew the first line would be something of a crib on Emily Brontë's "No coward soul is mine," because I'd already scribbled it down, "No battered hulk am I," but the rest would be D du M and nobody else. I would call it "The Old Ship," and later on give myself a break and have an afternoon's rabbiting with Adams. A good job I didn't have to worry about food, and could get an evening meal at the Ferry Inn. Curry and plum pudding. Scrumptious!

Everyone in the village was so friendly. I knew all their names by now. The Swigges, the Couches, the Bunneys, the Hunkins up the road, little Miss Roberts waving from her cottage, her macaw Robert calling "Rob, Rob" from the sea wall, old Captain Bate from across the harbour, who lent me a book called *Gypsy of the Horn* in which he had figured himself as the skipper. "He told

215

me I was a real shell-back, and I felt so proud. I think the greatest quality of this place is its peacefulness. It really is Fowey Haven, a blessed retreat for anyone who wants to be alone. I mean metaphorically, of course, because it's a very busy harbour, with the ships loading at the jetties, and plenty of noise going on all the time. Even a wet day doesn't matter, with the drizzle fanning my face, and the bracken red on the hills, and when it blows the air is alive with spray and salt. I watched Mr. and Mrs. Burghard going off to church in their Sunday clothes, Mr. B in a bowler hat, and I looked as dirty and as ragged as usual, thank God!''

I was careful, though, to wash and change the following Sunday, when invited to tea with the Quiller-Couches at their house, The Haven, in Fowey. I had no desire to cut a shabby figure before the great man and his family. "Lady 'Q,' their daughter Foy, an aunt, an old friend Mr. Phelps and a retired parson were there, and we sat down to a big tea in the dining-room. I thoroughly enjoyed myself, and liked Foy immensely. She loves the sea just as I do, and there was plenty to talk about. I stayed on after the others had gone. They belong here, if anyone does, and are Cornish to the last drop of their blood.''

The suggestion was made that instead of a motor launch I should own a sailing boat, and I told them this had already been discussed at Christmas, D having realised that *Cora Ann* was really only suited to the river or calm weather. In fact, Adams was making enquiries locally and further down the coast, and had heard of a craft known as a quay punt lying at St. Mawes which was for sale. The ''Qs'' even knew the owner.

The very next day Adams and I caught the train to Falmouth and went to inspect her. ''Her name is *Sanderling*,'' I reported, ''and she's almost as long as a pilotcutter. Ripping accommodation below, cabin sleeps four, fo'castle two, cockpit for engine, everything in splendid condition, paint all fresh. Adams and I can think of nothing else, though we found time to go over the *Cutty Sark*, berthed in

Falmouth, afterwards. She's a training ship now and a real beauty, but being winter carried no t'gallant yards nor royals. I wasn't a bit disappointed, though, and as for *Sanderling,* I'm in love with her!'' The arrangement with D had been that we would go shares in any sailing boat, and I would put up my half from the War Loan of £500 still in the bank. I wrote off at once to the owner, and joy of joys, on the very day I was summoned back to London, Adams came with a letter saying the owner was willing to sell. Leaving Fowey was the usual misery, but at least when I next returned he would greet me with *Sanderling.*

Happiness was short-lived. I had only been back at Cannon Hall a week when Adams wrote to say that the owner had changed his mind. He had decided, after all, not to sell.

''Oh, I'm so miserable. I don't know when I've felt so unhappy for a long time. Not since Phoebus was run over. I can't bear it. I just cry and cry. I wanted her so terribly, my beautiful ship. So many dreams of her I'd had. I just can't explain. . . . The family were very sweet about it, and said perhaps the owner would change his mind again, but it's no use. I sit and brood. I shall fall into one of my black February moods. Oh, my beautiful boat.''

There was small solace now in copying out the stories and poems I had written at Ferryside, and anyway the garage room at Cannon Hall was barred to me because Geoffrey had come to stay and was using it. Well, that was something. ''When the others go to bed I let him kiss me in the drawing-room. Funny, my first experience. I suppose I oughtn't to let him, but it was nice and pleasant. I wish he could have been more light-hearted about it, though, and then I would have no compunction. But men are so odd. It would be awful if he got properly keyed-up.''

Meg, Geoffrey's wife, was out of the nursing home and convalescing at Brighton. Possibly his excess of emotion was a symptom of relief. I did not enquire, and the kisses — never any more than that — continued. ''It seems so natural to kiss him now, and he is very sweet and lovable. The strange thing is it's so like kissing D. There is hardly any difference between them. Perhaps this family is the same as the Borgias. D is Pope Alexander, Geoffrey is Cesare, and I am Lucretia. A sort of incest. Except that kissing Geoffrey is more exciting, and it's fun creeping down late in my pyjamas, and him too, and saying goodnight.''

The ''shell-back'' admired by old Captain Bate, pulling down-harbour in her jersey and sea boots, seemed temporarily submerged, and the loss of the *Sanderling* forgotten in this growing rapport between cousins. Always an avid listener to adult confidences, I enjoyed hearing Geoffrey recount past love affairs — just as D did after Sunday supper — but, whereas D must be listened to without criticism, I would shake my head at Geoffrey and reprove him for bad behaviour and weakness of character. ''The thing is, I can think so clearly about him. I can see him through and through. One of these days I must talk straight to him, and make him promise to tell the truth, instead of always evading it, as he does to other people. I think I should have made a good sister, even if I do foolish things myself."

The straight talk turned into a straight letter, which I left for him to read, and the next day we lunched together in London and, as the saying goes, "had it out."

"The first glance at his face was enough. He'd understood every word of what I'd written. He told me it was absolutely uncanny how I knew him, every fault, every weakness I had got right. He said it was so wonderful it would never leave him, and it was going to help him tremendously. This was what I wanted, and I felt so good. We really talked seriously, without any silly business. I believe he is going to pull himself together. I make him promise not to go on being indefinite, not to be weak, not to take the easy way out, and above all not to lie, to me, to Meg, to anyone."

The reason for my insistence was that the following day Geoffrey was to sail for Australia, and it might be a year before I should see him again. My Borgia brother . . . What a strange relationship. And I would miss him. One of the last things he told me before he sailed was that D had questioned him about his feelings for me, inevitably in the dining room after Sunday supper.

"I've been in love with her for seven years."

"Nothing can come of it, you realise that?"

"I know, Uncle. I know."

End of conversation? It was the only report he gave me, but knowing how much D and Geoffrey were alike, in so many ways, I wondered whether perhaps they exchanged confidences of their young days with mutual understanding. As for myself, I was secretly relieved that nothing could ever "come of it," for a Borgia brother was one thing, a suitor, already married, was quite another. No entanglements for me. Strange, though, that when I was given an anaesthetic for the extraction of wisdom teeth at this time — the dentist came up to Cannon Hall to do it — and sudden oblivion descended, I heard someone groaning, "Daddy, Daddy!" through a mist, and it was myself emerging from the darkness. So it was not the Borgia brother but the Borgia father that the unconscious self demanded.

Godmother Billy, meanwhile, had taken off my various finished stories to be typed at the theatre. There were eleven of them altogether, and the idea was that when she had finished her task she would send them to the literary agent A. P. Watt for an opinion. I believe this was Viola's suggestion. Whatever the outcome, they were out of my hands now, and must take their chance.

No news from Adams about a boat. Geoffrey had sailed. My stories were at the theatre. So there was nothing to keep me in London. How much had I in the bank? Well, enough, and I decided to go to Paris and risk hard chairs with Fernande recounting my Borgia relationship with the departed Geoffrey. Besides, Paris in the spring, strolls in the *quartier italien,* the visit was overdue. . . . It started snowing as I left Dover, but who cared?

The pull of Paris was as strong as ever, and, despite the letters and cables that poured in from Cesare Borgia at every stopping place in the Mediterranean, the impact of his image faded as his liner steamed past Suez and into the Indian Ocean. I wrote, of course, and my letters would follow him to Melbourne, but I hoped he would keep his end of the correspondence as lighthearted and cheerful as I kept mine. His allusions to "the sacredness of our love" were slightly embarrassing, and reminded me of the writer Ethel M. Dell, whose novels he had so much admired. Fernande, though hardly sympathetic, did not scold. Australia, after all, was a long way off. And how pleasant it was to slip into the Boulogne routine, walks in the Bois and my favourite Italian Quarter. *"J'aime l'odeur des rues, du tabac, et de la bière — ça sent du pain bien cuit et de la poussière,"* says the diary. Strolls along the Seine towards St. Cloud had a good river smell, reminding me of Fowey, but somehow without heartache, without a sense of loss. A different kind of freedom.

We went to the lectures at the lycée, and to the theatre two or three times a week, while the thing I enjoyed most of all was sitting at a café watching people around me. "I have a sort of game I play, in which I try to remember faces of people in the streets and cafés, so vivid at the time, and it always happens that they pass out of my head about three minutes afterwards, nothing will stop them going. I wonder if subconsciously one remembers, and that accounts for the mass of faces I see when I close my eyes, or in dreams."

I was reading a lot again, which always happened when I stayed with Fernande, the novels of Willy, Colette, Georges Duhamel, with *Le Feu* by D'Annunzio thrown in for good measure.

Good news from home, when Godmother Billy forwarded me a letter from A. P. Watt saying they were pleased with my stories, and if I would write a few more they would have enough to submit for possible publication.

But — and this was not so good — Viola,

M and D had apparently gone with Ivor Novello to look at the silly film test I had done a year ago, and were much impressed. Viola even rang up from London about it, and told me there were plans for the two of us, with Ivor, to go to Budapest in the summer and do some film. A letter from M followed, full of this idea. Flattering, perhaps, but what about ties? I did not want to have a film career. "It would mean contracts, not being able to go away when I wanted to, no Fowey, no boats, and all for what? A little money and a lot of gush, and tiring tedious work. I'm not at all keen. Besides, it takes four days to get to Budapest, and four days back, all in a beastly train."

No, I wasn't going to be bounced into this, no matter what inducements. So fussing, too, having calls from London. D was the next to telephone, never having done it before. Why couldn't they all leave me alone? No, I would make my own plans. I would spend as much of the summer as I could down at Fowey, by myself, writing stories. Budapest and films were out.

"If my mind and soul live in Fowey," I thought, as I took the train once more from the Gare du Nord, "perhaps I leave my heart behind in Paris." I remembered a drawing of Grandpapa's in his *Peter Ibbetson,* where Peter stands on a wharf by London Bridge, watching the steamers start for Boulogne-sur-Mer. "I constantly haunted the docks," he wrote, "where the smell of tar and the sight of ropes and masts filled me with unutterable longings for the sea — for distant lands — for anywhere but where it was my fate to be."

Which was London. Poor Grandpapa. How he would have loved *l'odeur des rues* in the Italian Quarter in Boulogne-sur-Seine, and the harbour smells in Fowey. Such a waste he had to die before I was born. *"Rendez-moi les jours et les nuits qui n'existent plus,"* says the diary.

I arrived home in time for D and M's silver wedding, and there was something strangely touching about the occasion, because of the gifts they gave each other. M had gone to so much trouble to have her portrait painted, and the sad thing was that, as she uncovered it, we could see from his face he didn't care for it at all. It was not even a good likeness. Eager to produce his own present, he unwrapped a bracelet to put on her wrist. It was too small. "Oh dear, it was so pathetic. And yet slightly absurd and somehow perfect at the same time," says the diary, and when we three sisters had presented our parents with a huge potted azalea we all went off to a family celebration lunch at the Savoy.

Whether there was talk of Budapest, of a film future, goes unrecorded; but evidently the plan was put on one side, and forever. A week later I was down in Fowey, and apart from a couple of duty visits to London, and a brief trip to Paris at the end of July, I remained at Ferryside until mid-October.

Reunion with skipper Adams and dear fat Bingo was a joy, and I could tell from the smile on Adams' face that he had good news.

"I've been talking to Ernie Slade at his boatyard in Polruan," he told me, "and he says he and his brothers can build you a fishing lugger, same type as *Sanderling*, and for the price you were prepared to give for her. He's even got planking lying there ready to show you. What do you say?"

What did I say? I was ready to toss my sea boots in the air for excitement. The following morning I went to Polruan to meet Ernie Slade and discuss possibilities. It was true. He could do it. He knew of a piece of well-seasoned timber up Lerryn woods that would do for the ship's keel, and would tow it down the very next day.

"You'll be able to watch her building right from the start," he said, "and all going well, we'll have her launched by midsummer."

Thirty-two foot overall, twelve foot beam, five foot six inches depth, rigged as a yawl. No time for thinking out those stories for A. P. Watt, there was too much to do down at the yard, seeing the keel laid, watching the sawing of the planks, besides helping Adams to fit out *Cora Ann* for the coming season. Chatting with

Ernie Slade was interesting too, especially as he told me the old schooner *Jane Slade* was at last to be broken up, and how would we like to have the figurehead at Ferryside? Yes, she had been his gran all right, and his uncle Tom the skipper. I ought to go up Lanteglos churchyard and find her grave. I could hardly wait.

Yes, there it was, the family tombstone. Christopher Slade and his wife Jane Symons, died 1885, aged seventy-two. The original of the figurehead, my handsome Jane. Before long to be placed on the beam at Ferryside outside my window. Then Adams came along with a big box full of old papers and letters about the family. I went through them that very same evening, faded handwriting, going back to the early part of the nineteenth century. Ernie Slade supplied more information, and soon I was busy drawing out a genealogical table of the whole family, down to the present day. I couldn't get them out of my head. Was it my fancy, or was it true that Jane dominated them all, even after death — and she would be getting on when the schooner named after her was built?

"There's enough material here for a real book," I wrote in the diary, "though of course I should have to add a lot of imagination to it. Oh, I wonder if I shall ever have the energy to tackle such a big subject. Her son who was master of the ship would be very important, and there would be a great bond between mother and son. Ernie showed me the family Bible and I took copious notes. Jane had written down all her children's births in her own handwriting." Short stories were pushed aside, I could think of nothing but Jane Slade, and my own boat that her grandsons had started to build.

"I'm so glad my boat is to be built by a Slade," I told them.

What would we call our ship? I asked D, who sounded as enthusiastic about her as I was myself. He suggested *Marie-Louise,* after Aunt May. Yes, *Marie-Louise* was just right, and, what was more, it was French.

Then M, before returning with the others to London just before my twenty-first birthday, presented me with a thirteen-foot rowing boat, not for family use when they were all down but for myself alone. My cup of happiness was full. "She is painted black, and her name is *Annabelle Lee,* and there is a little red sail to go with her, just to hoist before the wind," I wrote on the birthday itself, "and as for being twenty-one, I'll leave it at that. I can't see that years make any difference, or days, or hours, it's things that happen to one that matter. I shan't look back. No guttering candles and dripping wicks for me. When I go let me go quickly, still a bright flame, no flickering! Meanwhile Adams and I celebrated my majority by taking *Annabelle Lee* out to sea and catching 13 pollock, which was a good start for the boat."

It was amusing opening the various family presents all alone, plus a book to write in from Viola, and a red neck'chief from Fernande, which would match the red sail in *Annabelle Lee*. While Geoffrey's first letter turned up from Melbourne.

"How unreal that month of February now seems. I shall always be devoted to him despite his many faults, but — *Je ne reconnais plus mes actions de jadis!*" Boats were more important than Borgia kisses after dark. . . .

Unfortunately, the brothers Slade did not fulfill their promise to have *Marie-Louise* ready by midsummer. There were to be various refinements, which for all my boasted knowledge of boats and seamanship were somewhat beyond me. A lead keel was to be fitted, she must be copper-fastened. The knocking and the hammering continued throughout July and August, and the only thing I felt competent enough to be consulted about was the placing of the W.C.

"You don't want'un anywhere where 'twould be awkward-like."

"No, Mr. Slade. That's right. Between fo'castle and cabins, then."

I wondered if Jane Slade had given similar orders when her schooner was being built. There wasn't much left of her ship now, she was stripped to her bare bones. The wheel had gone, the galley and deckhouse. Such waste and desolation, and the past seemed unreal when I pulled *Annabelle Lee* up Pont creek and climbed aboard her. I thought of all the family letters in the box, and how the schooner herself must have looked when she was painted and finished and launched. Now left abandoned, cold, and immeasurably old.

"My boat is in the same yard now. Where will she be, sixty years from now? Nothing is real. Not even the present. Sometimes life seems like a wall, pressing in upon one."

I had so hoped *Marie-Louise* would have been completed for when D was down for his August holiday, with the rest of the family and various friends, Bart Marshall, Edna Best and others; but although the actual launching did take place with D and myself on board, and I broke a bottle of champagne on the stern while the Slades and everyone cheered, she was not yet ready for sea. Visitors must rest content with fishing from *Cora Ann*.

Finally, on September 13th, the

great day dawned.

"A fine bright day, with a fairly strong easterly wind. I was so excited all morning I could hardly breathe. The first trip in *Marie-Louise*. I felt so nervous before going my knees nearly shook, not that I was frightened, but because it had come at last, and everything was new and strange and I don't think I could quite realise it all. All the men from Slade's yard came too, and we were soon under way, engine going, which we turned off outside the harbour. Then we felt the wind, and were away like a seagull riding the waves, the canvas filling. I took the tiller, I couldn't keep the smile off my face. It all went off splendidly, without a hitch, and I could see *Marie-Louise* was enjoying herself, and was just longing for a strong wind to kick about in. So passed her first trip. Angela was sick, and Bet felt bad, but there seemed no motion to me, or to Pat!" (Bet Hicks and Pat Wallace were staying at Ferryside.) "How glorious it was! One didn't think of anything, and yet felt terribly alive, and I loved the careless, contented expression of the men from Slade's. We were all together. It was *our* ship."

There were only a few weeks of sailing left before Adams told me the weather would soon be breaking, and we should strip her and lay her up before the autumn gales set in. One by one our visitors went back. M and Jeanne left the first day of October, and before she went M told me that if I could earn enough money to keep myself entirely there was no reason why I should not live at Ferryside as long as I liked. "Oh, God . . . I must concentrate, I must work, I'm hopelessly lazy and idle. If I go on like this I shall dream my life away. Life passes so relentlessly, and I shall only have myself to blame."

Angela and I had no more than a fortnight's respite before we too must return to London, and with *Marie-Louise* laid up we spent most of our time walking and exploring the countryside. I had by now discovered with fascination the enchanted woods on the Gribbin headland. "So like my Beacon poem, it's quite startling." And looking north, inland from the Gribbin, I could just make out the grey roof of a house there, set in its own grounds amongst trees.

Yes, Angela and I were told. That would be Menabilly. Belongs to Dr. Rashleigh, but he seldom lives there. A magistrate, comes down from Devon for Petty Sessions once a month. The Quiller-Couches gave further information: they used to visit it for garden parties in its heyday. And I gleaned snatches of family history. There was the lady in blue who looked, so it was said, from a side window, yet few had seen her face. There was the cavalier found beneath a buttress wall more than a hundred years ago. And there were the original sixteenth-century builders, merchants and traders; the Stuart royalists who suffered for their King; the Tory landowners with their white wigs and their broods of children; the Victorian landowners, with their rare plants and shrubs. I saw them all, in my mind's eye, down to the present owner, who could not love his home; and when I thought of him it was not of an elderly man, a respectable justice of the peace, but of a small boy orphaned at two years old, coming for his holidays in an Eton collar and tight black suit, watching his old grandfather with nervous, doubtful eyes.

"The drive is nearly three miles long, and overgrown," we were told. I for one was not to be deterred. The autumn colours had me bewitched from the start. So early one afternoon we set forth, Angela more reluctant, with her panting pekinese held by a leash. We came to the lodge at Four Turnings, as we had been instructed, and opened the creaking iron gates with the bluff and false courage common to the trespasser. The lodge was deserted. No one peered at us from the windows. We slunk down the drive, and were soon hidden by the shrubs and thick undergrowth.

The trees grew taller and more menacing. Yet still the drive led on, and never a house at the end of it. Suddenly Angela said, "It's after four . . . and the sun's gone." The pekinese watched her, pink tongue lolling. And then he stared into the bushes, pricking his ears at nothing. The first owl hooted. . . .

"I don't like it," said Angela firmly. "Let's go back."

"But the house," I said with longing, "we haven't seen the house."

She hesitated, and I dragged her on. But in an instant the day was gone from us. The drive had become a muddied path, leading to nowhere, and the shrubs, green no longer but a shrouding black, turned to fantastic shapes and sizes. I knew then that I was beaten. For that night only.

"All right," I said grudgingly, "we'll find the house another time."

We struck off through the trees and came out upon the hillside. In the distance below us stretched the sea. Behind us lay the woods and the valley through which we had come. But nowhere was there a sign of any house. Nowhere at all.

"Perhaps," I thought to myself, "it is a house of secrets, and has no wish to be disturbed." But I knew I should not rest until I had found it.

The following day we tried another approach, taking M's little car and driving to the west lodge, leaving the car at the gate. We walked across the park and through another gate, and came to the house. Grey, still, silent. The windows were shuttered fast, white and barred. Ivy covered the grey walls and threw tendrils round the windows. It was early still, and the house was sleeping. But later, when the sun was high, there would come no wreath of smoke from the chimneys. The shutters would not be thrown back, nor the doors unfastened. No voices would sound within those darkened rooms. Menabilly would sleep on, like the sleeping beauty of the fairy tale, until someone should come to wake her.

We watched awhile in silence, and then, emboldened, walked across the lawn and stood beneath the windows. She was a two-storied house, and with the ivy off her would have a classic austerity that her present shaggy covering denied her.

One of her nineteenth-century owners had taken away her small-paned windows and given her plate glass instead, and he had also built at her northern end an ugly wing that conformed ill with the rest of her. But with all her faults she had a grace and charm that made me hers upon the instant. She was, or so it seemed to me, bathed in a strange mystery. She held a secret — not one, not two, but many — that she withheld from many people but would give to one who loved her well.

One family only had lived within her walls. One family who had given her life. They had been born there, they had loved, they had quarreled, they had suffered, they had died. And out of these emotions she had woven a personality for herself, she had become what their thoughts and their desires had made her.

And now the story was ended. She lay there in her last sleep. Nothing remained for her but to decay and die. Menabilly, haunting, mysterious . . . "The place has taken hold of me," I wrote in the diary. "I must go back there next time I come down."

Next time? But when? In the train, London-bound, impressions fought for supremacy. "The lights of Polruan and Fowey. Ships anchored, looming up through blackness. The jetties, white with clay. Mysterious shrouded trees, owls hooting, the splash of muffled oars in lumpy water, Menabilly . . . All I want is to be at Fowey. Nothing and no one else. This, now, is my life."

Apprenticeship

If I had known I should not see Fowey again until mid-April of the following year I believe I should have caught the next train back. As it was, even a fortnight at Hampstead was enough.

"It's no use. I *must* make money and be independent, but how can I ever make enough? Even if my stories are published they can only bring in a very little, and though I might hack away at articles for magazines or newspapers, they might not be willing to print them. I *won't* go on the films, that would merely be slaving to no purpose, for I should never have time for anything else. I think I've been born into the wrong atmosphere. Take Sunday, so typical of all the Sundays I have ever known. People to lunch, to tea, to dinner, and endless discussion of plays, of actors, and criticism of everything. I have to become an unnatural Sunday person and be part of it all. The real me is at Fowey in my boat, alone. Not London, and everyone fussing, and having to buy clothes. All I want is Fowey, and now and then going to Paris to see Fernande. I'm selfish, and admit it, but I know that no person will ever get into my blood as a place can, as Fowey does. People and things pass away, but not places."

Angela and Jeanne were content with their lives. Why did I have to be different? We three got on so well, we never quarrelled, and could discuss every subject under the sun; yet they had no desire to break away, as I did. Nor could I complain that life at home was restricted to walks on the heath, when I could go into London as often as I pleased, to films, to matinées, to see old friends like my Camposena roommate Doodie or the Wallaces — but this simply filled in time, time that should have been spent in Fowey, working, either on short stories or upon a boat.

The "I read also" for the autumn is a pointer to the mood within. *Practical Seamanship, Studies in Navigation, Round the Horn Before the Mast,* and interposed between them a curiosity by a Frenchman, Camille Nauclair, entitled *L'Amour Physique.*

It was perhaps a little of the last that I needed to jolt me out of despondency, lighten the drudgery of copying my stories in ink so that Billy could type them and give some of them to be read by no less a person than Uncle Willie Beaumont, her brother, who was editor of *The Bystander.* The agent A. P. Watt having had no success so far, perhaps Uncle Willie might even publish one or two in his popular weekly magazine. It would be a start.

I reckoned without the editorial blue pencil, however, for although Uncle Willie professed himself delighted with the story about the fashionable vicar, "And Now to God the Father," he told me it would have to be cut considerably to suit the required length. Payment ten guineas. So how about it? Oh no . . . not cut down, all subtlety gone, in my opinion ruined, and all to have ten quid in the pocket. No, Uncle Willie, no. He laughed over the telephone, he was not offended, and told me all the stories were good and he would consider publishing them, printed in full. I must wait and see, though. When he had the space. Back, then, to *Studies in Navigation,* of which I didn't understand a word. I'd never make a navigator, it was all deviations and variations and double angles. "Oh, I'm sick of my unhealthy lassitude, which comes from yawning over a fire, or breathing the stifling air in the tube, wearing tight hats and stupid shoes. I ought to be on the top of a cliff, running and running, and drinking in great draughts of sky, and grass, and sea."

I must have spilt some of this frustration on to Pat Wallace, for, unexpectedly, there came an invitation from Edgar and Jim to be one of their party at Caux for the New Year. There was to be no Christmas at Fowey, so I could hardly wait. The sun, the snow, the mountains — next best thing to Cornwall.

Caux turned out to be even better than the previous time two years before. I considered I possessed greater savoir-faire at twenty-one than I had at nineteen. I was more proficient at the sports, skating, luging, skiing, and on more equal terms with all my contemporaries. We were a happy crowd at the Caux Palace Hotel that January of 1929, and for the first time in my life I found the young men flocking. *L'amour physique?* Well, hardly. But dancing cheek to cheek, kisses in the bar, tottering up to bed at 4 A.M., where Pat and I boasted of our conquests until we fell asleep.

"I was kissed by two young men at the same time," I told Fernande in one letter, "and another man, married, kissed me outside in the snow."

Horrified at my misconduct, she wrote a warning letter to Godmother Billy — I had not realised they shared confidences — who repeated the tale to the family at Cannon Hall, and by the time the Wallaces returned home to London, dropping me off in Paris on the way, the story had been exaggerated to such an extent that it appeared to be the general belief that I had cast my favours amongst every available male in the hotel. Dear Edgar's affection for me and his confidence in my behaviour were considerably shaken, and despite the vehement denials of his daughter Pat that anything serious had ever occurred I was, for several months, no longer *persona grata* in their family circle.

In retrospect, how naïve were we all, young and middle-aged alike, in 1929! Kisses in the bar, and in the snow. It was really shocking. And when a French count — one of the cheek-to-cheek dancing partners — turned up at Boulogne-sur-Seine with a bouquet of flowers for me and an invitation to dinner, Fernande's face was a study, as she sat bolt upright in her salon to receive him!

"Disappointing," I noted in the diary. "Fred wore a dreary suit and talked to us about big game in Africa. How different from Caux, where he looked so attractive in a dinner-jacket. It makes me feel like retiring to a hut and reading philosophy."

Instead, I went home at the end of February, having thrown aside my Swiss exuberance under the watchful eye of Fernande, who suggested that a little hard work would be beneficial for a change; and despite the somewhat cool reception from the family, still suspicious about those kisses in the bar of the Caux Palace Hotel, I was pleased to announce in my diary that "the restless energy has left my body and gone into my mind and thoughts, and I'm just on fire to write, and write in the same way that I was on fire to ski, and luge, and do things swiftly. I'd got an idea for an actress story, in several episodes, and sat down at first with a blank mind, and then, suddenly, it was like switching on an electric light in my brain and the hours absolutely fled." The story took about a fortnight to compose and then copy out in ink, and when finished the inevitable reaction set in; emptiness, boredom, and an odd sort of melancholy too.

"I strolled down the garden, and passed Jock's grave. I can never think of him without a pain, nor of Brutus, nor

Phoebus. Perhaps they were children I had in a past life, and shall never have in this. Or maybe once I was cruel to animals and am paying for it this time. The thought of Death suddenly hit me in the face. However one lives, whatever one does, death can't be prevented. The inevitability of one's body rotting to dust one day. We are all shadows. Tomorrow, and tomorrow, and tomorrow . . . I must stop this mood and study navigation."

It wasn't necessary. One of my followers at Caux telephoned and asked me out to dinner. No Frenchman with a bouquet, but the young man whom I secretly liked the best, one of the Wallace party who worked for Edgar at his film studio, Carol, tall, slim-hipped, and twenty-two. "I don't know what there is about that boy, but I can't help loving him a bit." More than a bit. Soon we were going out two or three times a week, depending upon the studio work he had on hand. Dinner first, a film afterwards, and then supper of eggs and bacon in the gallery of the Kit-Kat, and a zigzag drive round London in his battered Morris before I was dropped at home. Never the conventional outing. No dancing, no evening clothes. And if we gave the Kit-Kat a miss, then it would be a pavement coffee stall and a ham sandwich apiece.

"We drive crazily along the Watford by-pass. We climb the scaffolding up the roof to a half-built house, clinging to each other, laughing. We played, and fought, and fooled. Oh, it's fun being young sometimes."

And later. "I'm sleeping in the garage-room because Jeanne is in bed with a temperature, and a nurse is there. I opened the window of the loft and talked to Carol after I'd let myself in. He wanted to do a Douglas Fairbanks and climb up to me, but hadn't the courage of his ideas! It would have been awful, I suppose, if he'd been seen. As it is, my going out with him in the evenings like this is causing much discussion in the family. Honestly! They might have been born centuries ago. They treat me like a Victorian miss of 16, instead of being nearly 22."

Alexander Borgia was on the warpath again, sessions after Sunday supper becoming grim.

"Are you in love with Carol?"

"He's a dear. I'm fond of him."

"Is he serious?"

"I don't know what you mean by serious."

"Where do you go when the restaurants have closed?"

"We . . . sort of drive around."

What on earth did D think we did? He wouldn't understand if I explained that on Wednesday after dinner we drove down to Limehouse and the docks, and explored a beach by the river where a Thames barge was anchored. Ideas here for stories. A boy like Carol leaving home and running away to sea. Or was the boy myself? A mixture of both, perhaps. How strange.

"This coming home at one in the morning has got to stop. In future you must be home by midnight. Really, it's the thin end of the wedge." M in the morning, her eyes cold. The thin end of the wedge. Why did there have to be such a drama? You'd think they would be pleased that I had a young man of my own at last. Nothing I did was ever right.

"I copy out a story I started ages ago called 'East Wind.' Few people will read it or like it. There's no conversation at all, a few scattered sentences. I don't know if I've caught the atmosphere or not. It's sordid, perhaps, brutal, and essentially primitive. What a pity I'm not a vagrant on the face of the earth. Wandering in strange cities, foreign lands, open spaces, fighting, drinking, loving physically. And here I am, only a silly sheltered girl in a dress, knowing nothing at all — but Nothing."

What a relief to be going to Fowey in three days' time. One last evening with Carol, supper, and the East India docks; then the drive home, our eyes on the clock, just time to put our arms around each other and kiss for five minutes before Christ Church clock struck midnight.

"Shall I call you up, darling, at Fowey?"

"Yes, please."

Oh dear, how sad, the old Morris clanking away up Cannon Place, and was that a curtain moving on the top landing at home, and someone hovering behind it? If so, Alexander Borgia was back early from the theatre. Damn.

"It's odd that one comes into being at all. Twenty-six years ago D and M were married, and what have I to do with this, and their lives in particular? Here I am, a separate being, only myself. I wonder if happiness will always elude me, lying just ahead, round the corner. What it is, I shall never discover. And death, all the while, waiting like a mocking shadow."

Yet, once in Fowey, the mocking shadow was half a century away. "Oh, the utter joy of looking across the harbour once again. Blue smoke curling from the grey houses opposite, the haze over the water, the noise and smell of ships. Adams smiling, disappearing in the *Cora Ann. Annabelle Lee* at her moorings. The villagers looking over Bodinnick wall. What more on earth should I want but these things? I'm here, I've always been here, and yet the me of the past is still going on. The past me is kissing Carol, greeting Fernande in Paris, kneeling at prayer in Camposena, standing on the heath with the dogs, playing cricket in knickers on the lawn. All this continues side-by-side, separately, having nothing to do with the present. And also the future, whatever it may hold in store, I am doing it at this moment. I mustn't think any more, or I shall tie myself in knots."

Two days later I trespassed once again in the grounds of Menabilly. The place called to me. I felt I just had to peep at the house, if only for a moment. I did a thing I had never done before — I rose at 5 A.M., pulled across the harbour in my pram, walked through the sleeping town, and climbed out on the cliffs just as the sun himself climbed out of Pont hill behind me. The sea was glass. The air was soft and misty warm. And the only other creature out of bed was a fisherman, hauling crab pots, at the harbour mouth. It gave me a fine feeling of conceit, to be up before the world. I came down to Pridmouth bay, passing the solitary cottage by the lake, and, opening a small gate, saw a narrow path leading to the woods. Now, at last, I had the day before me, and no owls, no shadows could turn me back.

I followed the path to the summit of the hill and then, emerging from the woods, turned left, and found myself upon a high grass walk, with all the bay stretched out below me and the Gribbin Head beyond. The morning mist was lifting, and the sun was coming up above the trees. This time there was no owl, but blackbird, thrush and robin greeting the summer day.

I edged my way on to the lawn, and there she stood. My house of secrets. My elusive Menabilly . . .

I sat and stared at the windows. The caretaker, who must come from the lodge to air the house, had pulled back a blind, showing a chink of space, and presently, venturing across the lawn and pressing my face to the window, I could catch a glimpse of the room within. It must be a dining room. Dark panels, a sideboard, a forgotten corkscrew lying upon it, a great fireplace. And on the walls the family portraits stared into the silence and the dust. Another room, bare of blinds, in the eastern wing, had once been a library, judging by the books upon the shelves, but was now a lumber place, and in the centre of it stood a great dappled rocking horse with scarlet nostrils. What little blue-sashed children had once bestrode his back? Where was the laughter gone? Where were the voices that had called along the passages? I could not know that in fourteen years' time, married, with three children, it was their voices I should hear calling through the house, that my own furniture would fill the rooms, and that all this would somehow be a sequel to a novel I should write in 1937 - 38 and call *Rebecca* — Menabilly itself fusing with the childhood memory of Milton.

I cannot recollect, now, how long I wandered round and stared at the house. It was past midday, perhaps, when I returned to the living world, empty, lightheaded, with no breakfast inside me. I must be practical. Forget the past. Forget that house of secrets. *Marie-Louise* must be fitted out, *Cora Ann* have a coat of varnish, there was so much to do — it left little time for dreaming, or for work.

"I don't seem to be able to concentrate

257

on working just yet, but somewhere, at the back of my mind, not developed, still in embryo, scarcely born in thought, is the novel I want to write about Jane Slade. I probably shan't write it until I'm forty. It's got to be prepared, over months, and I know I'm not ready for it yet. A soft rain fell today, and a sort of happy melancholy came upon me. I walked up to the Castle point, and it seemed to me that I was standing on the cliffs years hence with a grown-up son, but of course I was only a ghost, being long dead, existing only in his thoughts. And from that I passed on to thinking of my unborn book about Jane, and I knew it must be the story of four generations."

Past and future linked, confusing me, and then when I returned to Ferryside it would be to have a telephone call from Carol, or a scrap of a letter saying, "Darling Daph, how are you, when are you coming back?" No more than this ever, he was hopeless at letters. Or, more disturbing still, a letter from Geoffrey, home from Australia, separated now from Meg and on his own.

"Oh, I've had such a miserable letter from Geoffrey. I'm quite overcome. Forty-three, living alone in rooms, no one wanting him, his money going, out of a job, no prospects of one, and the ahead of him absolutely blank. The time when a man wants to be settled, having a wife and home, and he, through his own fault largely, has wasted his life, yet must face the future somehow. It's too terrible, not only for him, but for all the lonely weak people in the world. It makes me want to open my arms and give them everything, but what do I do but pull a boat and whistle a tune? I *must* think more humanely in future. I suddenly understand Christianity for the first time, but will it alter me, make me less selfish? No, of course not. I know myself too well."

In less than a week the mood had changed once more. Perhaps it was because M and Granny were down for ten days, so that I was aware of loss of liberty.

"I'm rapidly coming to the conclusion that freedom is the only thing that matters to me at all. Also utter irresponsibility! Never to have to obey any laws or rules, only certain standards one sets for oneself. I want to revolt, as an individual, against everything that 'ties.' If only one could live one's life unhampered in any way, not getting in knots and twisting up. There must be a free way, without making a muck of it all.''

My twenty-second birthday came and, M and Granny having departed, I spent it alone as I had done the preceding year.

"Oh dear . . . I shall never be twenty-one again. It's supposed to be the best year of one's life. Never more. . . . Well, it's been pretty good for me. But perhaps I felt like this at twelve, and one soon forgets, and that's the tragedy. It poured with rain all day, so I couldn't get out, but I spent the afternoon cutting out idiotic things from the newspaper to send to Carol. Presents from family, mostly for *Marie-Louise,* and a lovely pair of binoculars from D. I appreciate this gratefully.''

Uncle Willie had come forward with a gesture too. He had printed ''And Now to

God the Father'' in the current *Bystander,* and, though shortened by the editorial blue pencil, it was pleasant to see myself in print at last. I went self-consciously into the W. H. Smith's in Fowey and bought a copy, hoping the girl behind the counter did not know why I was getting it.

"Pity it's been so cut, but it doesn't look too bad. I hope Uncle Willie pays up with that ten quid!"

I celebrated my first sale by a play on words, since it was the first sail of the season in *Marie-Louise.* We trawled off Polperro and caught nothing, but that didn't matter. "Utter peace comes upon me when out to sea. No cares, no feelings, no restlessness, no repressions; just calm, with scarcely a thought." And a few days later I landed a seven-pound pollock, with Adams grinning from ear to ear. Then the inevitable summons to return to Hampstead.

"I sat for a long while at the open hatch by the slip watching the harbour. I felt absolutely pure, like a soul at rest. It seemed to me that everything I looked upon was beautiful and eternal, and that no trace of anything was ever lost. I pondered for a long while on Jane Slade and the four generations. There must be no unworthy line. But shall I ever be in a fit state to write it?"

Obviously not yet, for back at Hampstead the drama of the ordinary non-writing life awaited me. Geoffrey was home, hoping to resume the Cesare Borgia relationship, which indeed I did not mind in moderation, but since I had found Carol things were rather different. Carol and I had dinner together the very first evening after my return, and, "He's looking very thin and pale, but is such a darling, what shall I do? We talk and talk for ages, and of course it got late and we had to dash home in case M was cross. I think I do love him, but not a 'swept off my feet' thing, more a sort of tugging maternal feeling. Whereas Geoffrey, whom I saw for lunch, and who is looking well and fit, is still a brother. Brother and son. Such a muddle."

A muddle indeed. The confusion of

London life set in with a vengeance, from news in the daily paper and on the wireless to happenings at home.

"The King is ill again, the Socialists are winning after the General Election yesterday, D apparently owes thousands for income tax and has no play to hand. Angela has got to have her appendix out, Fernande has to find a new house in Paris, Geoffrey is without a job, and although I want to write and write and write, I keep thinking about Carol. How will it all end?"

Not with living upon the £10 from *The Bystander*. My ally Uncle Willie introduced me to Miss Nancy Pearn, of the literary agency Curtis Brown, and I handed over the rest of my short stories in the hope that she might be able to place some of them. The outings with Carol continued, and when matinées and evening performances kept him at the Shaftesbury Theatre I would sit in his room, waiting for the performance to end, or take myself off to a film alone until he could join me.

"What is there about him that crumples

me up? His extreme youth, I suppose, though he is five months older than me. I sat in his room during the matinée, and he kept leaping up there from the stage to kiss me, and then dashing down again. So lovable and childish. But he's so good to talk to as well. We can discuss everything, or else just drive along in his car without speaking a word. It's something about being together."

More drama, though. One night, after supper at the Café Anglais, I wasn't home until after 1 A.M., and was greeted with a stony face from M the next morning.

"M says she has had enough. It was the last time I should be late. And she's written to Carol to tell him so. She wouldn't tell me what she had said. Suppose she has written something terrible? This of course has finished me for the day. I know it was bloody of me to be late when they are worried about Angela's appendix, but I wasn't thinking about that at the time."

Carol, scarlet with embarrassment, wrote a polite note of apology in return. He promised it wouldn't happen again.

But oh, it would mean dashing out of the theatre in the evening to get me home, no time for . . . well, anything.

"Darling, if only I earned enough money we could get married," he said.

"Yes, but then I should never get down to Fowey."

"That's true, that's true. Where the hell would we live?"

"It's no good. It wouldn't work. Don't let's think about it."

Seize the passing moment, hold on to it, make it last, at least until midnight. After that, *qu'importe?* Perhaps we should both die.

Death, however, was not imminent; instead an invitation from Rudolf Kommer, whom Viola and I had met in Berlin in 1927, to join him and a select party, our host the millionaire Otto Kahn, in a steam yacht cruising to the Norwegian fjords at the end of June.

My immediate impulse was to refuse. I wouldn't know anyone but Kommer, it would mean buying new clothes, panic set in, but the pressure was insistent. Such a wonderful opportunity, said the family, it would never occur again, I would be mad not to go, and what about all my talk of loving the sea? The idea was off, then on again, and finally, putting a brave face on it, suitcases packed, good-byes said to Carol, I met my fellow guests at Victoria Station, destination Hamburg, where we were to join the yacht.

It did not occur to me then, or indeed later, that the invitation, though doubtless genuine enough, had its origins in a scheme devised by D, Viola and Rudolf Kommer to lure me away to new scenes, new people, and so from the dressing room at the Shaftesbury Theatre and Carol. Nor, perhaps, did it strike M and D that if, as they believed, I had misconducted myself when under the protection of Edgar Wallace and his wife Jim at the Caux Palace Hotel, I might be doubly vulnerable to temptation in the narrow confines of a yacht amongst a group of people whom they themselves had never met, and with whom, as it turned out, my host Otto Kahn and his friend Rudolf Kommer had only a slight acquaintance! The ways of parents were indeed strange in the 1920s. An opportunity, right enough, but for what?

We were certainly a mixed bunch who gathered on Victoria platform, eyeing one another with dubious expectancy. A wing commander and his attractive wife, two married ladies minus their husbands, two unattached males, one big and cheerful, the other silent, reserved, bearded like Tennyson. Who, I wondered, would pair off with whom? If pushed, I'd plump for Tennyson. Competition not likely to be strong.

Kommer and our host met us in Hamburg, where the tenth member of the party also joined us, a beautiful German girl, whom I took to be the perquisite of mine host — apparently he had met her for the first time a few nights previously. Despite a sleepless night in the train, which had arrived at Hamburg at 8:30 A.M., the port and all the shipping made my day, especially when I spotted one of the ships that regularly came to load china clay in Fowey. Then off to join the steam yacht *Albion*.

"Well," says the diary, "about the most

luxurious thing I've ever seen afloat. Great open decks, and every stateroom with a bathroom attached. Drawing-room, dining-room, and we all sat down to a marvellous lunch, setting off for sea immediately afterwards. Everyone very nice."

So far so good. We were all getting acquainted. Copenhagen, Visby, Stockholm, impressions crowding, not so much of my companions as of the places visited, and at Stockholm especially the white twilight that never darkened, and the demoralising fact that at midnight came the dawn. I thought of the boy who ran away to sea in the book I must write one day, but he wouldn't be in a steam yacht, he'd be sailing before the mast. Then a jerk back to the present. "I must say Otto Kahn is a wonderful person. I love his theories and his philosophy of life. Actually I think he is transferring his affection from Irene [the German beauty] to me. But I'm beginning to do quite well with Tennyson, dragging him slowly from his shell. But I wish he'd shave off his beard."

Oslo made no great impression upon me. The fjords were another matter. "This beauty is too much. It's defeating, utterly bewildering. Beauty most exquisite. Blue and ice-white water, rushing, foaming, throbbing, and the mountains high and aloof with green, thick trees, yet utterly desolate, no humanity. Somehow, profoundly unhappy. The fjord is too narrow, closing in upon one."

The sense of depression passed. The next thing I knew I was sitting beside my host on the banks of a fjord, nobody else present, and, his attentions becoming rather marked, I wondered how to repel them without seeming ungracious.

"What a glorious day! I must have a swim," I announced, and, springing to my feet, stripped off my clothes and plunged naked into the water before his astonished eyes. A daring manoeuvre, but it worked. He was in his sixties, and did not attempt to follow my example. The attentions were more muted afterwards, although, being a generous host, he offered to buy me a fur coat at a gift shop at the head of another fjord. This I declined, asking for a dagger instead, and the same dagger reposes on my desk today. One never knows when it might come in useful.

As the yacht turned south once more, so the weather became rough, and with it attitudes altered. "I think we are all getting on one another's nerves. Kommer hasn't spoken to me for two days, I don't know why. The women are on edge. Irene got blind drunk at lunch. She's lovely to look at but such a crashing bore, perhaps that's why Kahn went off her and the other men didn't fall. As for George [the wing commander] he is at this moment lying on my bed, purely to rag, as the poets would say! As long as he doesn't start snoring I don't care."

The Caux Palace Hotel was certainly a kindergarten compared to the *Albion.* By the time we arrived back in Hamburg the wing commander had been called to order by his wife, Tennyson was making dates with me for dinner-for-two in London, and the only male member of the party who had remained cheerfully aloof through the whole cruise was the big fellow, Ralph, but perhaps this was because his whole attention had been centred upon a book he was reading entitled *The Sexual Life of Savages*.

Friday, July 12th. "Well, it's over. Three weeks of hectic living coming to an abrupt end, and people who have lived in a block together all parting and shaking hands on a platform. I must write my thanking letter to Kahn. Difficult thing to do as I hate being obvious in any form or fashion."

A genuine welcome awaited me at home. "What a wonderful time you must have had! So kind of Otto Kahn to have invited you." No charges of misconduct. Rudolf Kommer must have reported well of my behaviour, as well he might, despite the scalps dangling from my belt, and Tennyson's accusation that I had spoilt the cruise for the other women. In fact, my conduct had been irreproachable. A little horseplay, neither more nor less, and how relaxing it was to sit once more in the dressing room at the Shaftesbury Theatre and watch Carol remove his make-up in front of the mirror.

"Did you have fun, darling?"

"Yes, in a way. But not like this."

Which was true. And he asked no questions. Just smiled, boyishly, in his inimitable way, a happy, mutual trust between us. He would be off, before many weeks, on tour with Edgar's play *The Calendar,* and there were not many evenings ahead for us to spend together. Also, for some reason now forgotten, there was no plan for myself or for the family to go down to Fowey before September. So what to do? Fernande and Paris were the only answer. August in London an impossibility. First I had a date with Michael Joseph, who ran the book side of Curtis Brown, and he told me that I ought to write a novel before thinking of publishing my short stories. Had I any idea in mind? Yes, but I wasn't ready for it yet. I had to get right away from everybody, settle alone at Fowey, and leave myself absolutely clear to get on with it. It must be untouched by any outside influence. Did he understand? Curiously enough, he did.

"All right," he said, "do some short

stories first, if that's how you feel. Then we'll see."

Brewing up for an inevitably heavy cold, which I disguised from everyone at home, I set forth for Paris, drugged with quinine, on July 25th, and was immediately put to bed with a hot water bottle by the anxious Fernande, who pronounced my excessive fatigue as quite clearly the result of the Scandinavian cruise, of which she most obviously heartily disapproved.

"Fernande talks to me about myself, things perhaps I knew, but had shut away in a convenient corner. I believe all she said to me was true in every sense. But it's all so difficult. The writing me is different from the living me, yet they're both mixed up. If writing goes there would be no longer any reason for living. It's the opposite extremes that makes the conflict."

"Your basic character is weak," she told me, "like your cousin Geoffrey."

"It's not, it's not," I insisted, and, outraged that she should consider me some sort of flotsam, drifting with the current, I thought of the many stories waiting to be written, the novel about Jane Slade still lying beneath the surface. "One day you will be proud of me," I said, "you wait, one day . . ."

My cold got worse. I had a stiff neck into the bargain. I read *La Fin de Maupassant* and saw myself going mad as he had done, then turned to my loved Katherine Mansfield for consolation, but she also had a sad ending to her life.

"We must somehow get to Fontainebleau," I said, "and find her grave."

Fernande promised. We could stay at Barbizon and visit it from there, but first I would have to get rid of the cold, and she must see lawyers and bank manager about a new house — her present home in Boulogne-sur-Seine was proving too small, and pupils were at last increasing — but there were various difficulties, though I did not enquire the details.

Ideas for stories began to crowd thick and fast, like people waiting for a train. A face in a street, a face in a café, never anyone I knew, and nothing to do with the

Scandinavian cruise or my own experiences, but I could see these people, picture their lives. I sat down in the little salon, armed with a new fountain pen, and began to write. "Salle d'Attente," "Maisie," "Peace." "It's funny," I noted in the diary, "how often I seem to build a story around one sentence, nearly always the last one, too. The themes are a bit depressing but I just can't get rid of that."

Finally, in mid-August, Fernande decided upon a house in Neuilly. Old-fashioned, only two bathrooms, but a garden, a tennis court, and bedrooms for as many as sixteen girls. I wondered how in the world Fernande would manage, but a hurried visit to the bank decided her.

"Now can we go to Barbizon?"

"*Allons-y.*"

She must have been more flush of cash than I realised, for we hired the nice local taxi driver in Boulogne, who drove us all the way, and deposited us at the Hotel de la Forêt for a week. It was lovely and peaceful after the heat of Paris, and although Barbizon, with its many artistic associations with Millet and others, including my own R. L. Stevenson, was already a tourist centre and full of Americans and char-à-bancs during the day, we had only to walk a little way and find ourselves in the depths of the cool forest.

The highlight, for me at any rate, was the visit to find Katherine Mansfield's grave at Fontainebleau, so long planned.

"We discovered the *cimetière* on a hill. The *gardien* told us that she was first buried in the *fosse commune* — the common grave for the poor — but her *beau-frère* had her moved and placed where she is now, with just a plain slab stone in memory. Her husband, Middleton Murry, had never been near it. I bought some flowers and put them on her grave. I wish I had the money to pay for it to be kept in order. I can't forget it."

I knew by now that she had lived so near to us at Cannon Hall, and watched us as children, and I wondered if, now dead, she understood how much her stories meant to me, and how dearly I wished that I could write as well as she had done.

Two days only in Paris before going home, and it was sad to leave the little house in Boulogne which I should never see again, and wave the inevitable good-bye at the Gare du Nord to Fernande, faced with the move to Neuilly within a month. Dear Schüller would benefit at least, with a fenced-in kennel and run in one corner of the large garden, and walks in the Bois as close as they had been in Boulogne.

"Toujours les départs, from someone or from something. And Carol is in Manchester. I am just someone sitting in a train reading a paper without feelings or emotion, journeying without incident."

Twenty-four hours in London and then, thank heaven, Fowey once more. But first a quick visit to Michael Joseph of Curtis Brown to hand over the stories written in Paris, and to hear his opinion of the others I had left with him. "He was very fair, but liked 'Portrait of an Actress' best, which I think is strange, I'm sure he's wrong." Uncle Willie said the same. Yet I hadn't felt the actress story in the way I had felt the others. Perhaps feelings didn't come into it where agents and editors were concerned.

A hilarious lunch with Geoffrey, no longer Cesare Borgia but a genuine brother, a glance at the rehearsal of *Dear Brutus,* which D was to revive, a call on the Wallaces in Portland Place, and I was all set for Cornwall and *Marie-Louise.*

The novel of Jane Slade was brewing steadily at the back of my mind, but there was no hope of getting down to it for another month, for Ferryside was full of family and friends coming in relays. Ah well, never mind. Sailing, swimming and exploring would occupy the day. More trespassing at Menabilly, my fellow conspirators on this occasion Cousin Ursula, Uncle Willie's daughter, Jeanne and her school friend Elaine. We started from the lodge gates again, the east one at Four Turnings, and like last year with Angela plunged forever along that dark sinister drive, overgrown and tangled. I thought we should never reach the house, but we finally did, coming upon the northern addition, which faced directly upon the woods. To our amazement we were able to shift one of the windows, and the four of us crept in, dropping softly upon the dusty floor. Dust everywhere, and the silence of death. We stared around us at cobwebbed walls. In the corners were great fungus growths, coloured a livid brown. Then stealthily we found our way along a passage, dark and murky, through a lamp room, with more dust, more debris, and finally to the main part of the house, which before I had only glimpsed through chinks in the shutters from the lawn outside.

At last. At last . . . I had imagined it so often. Here were the rooms, leading one out of another; the staircase, with the faded crimson wall, and above it a finely moulded ceiling; portraits forever, staring down upon us. Did they resent intrusion? Shiny chintz sofas and chairs in the long drawing room on the ground floor, with water colours on the white panels, and the forgotten corkscrew still lay upon the sideboard of the dark-panelled dining room. Was the silence of it all too much for the owner, so that when he came to Cornwall once a month for

Petty Sessions he preferred, so they said, to stay in Par, in one of the small almshouses his grandfather had built?

The silence and the shadows were too much for us as well, and we turned and found our way back to the unfurnished north wing, passing on our way the library that still housed the leather-bound books and the dappled rocking horse. We climbed out of the window, and, being the last to leave, I made sure it was closed securely as the others wandered off. From a broken pane on the floor above my head came a great white owl, who flapped his way into the woods and vanished.

Much chatter and discussion as we made the long trek home, but it was hard to shake off the haunting impression the house had made upon me. If only someone could live there and bring it back to life, someone with children, the sound of laughter and happiness once more. And why did a past that I had never known possess me so completely? The people who had lived and died here once at Menabilly . . . the people who had built and sailed *Jane Slade* at Polruan, then left her to rot on the beach . . . the tumble-down cottage in a deserted plum orchard, which we came upon during another expedition. All that remained were the walls, two windows and a hearth. Once, perhaps, two hundred years ago, a woman had bent over that same hearth and stood at the window, watching. Now the tide was out, there were long flat stretches of mud, and only a narrow channel of water. Mournful, mournful. I wanted to be alone, but the others would laugh and talk. Always the past, just out of reach, waiting to be recaptured. Why did I feel so sad thinking of a past I had never known?

More cheerful moods out sailing. "The tiller was kicking under me like an impatient high-spirited horse, and the ship leant over with her lee-rail awash. My arms ached with the strain. There was a hissing sound of the wind in the mainsail, the creaking of masts and shrouds. Grey sea, grey sky, the wind coming in little fierce gusts and sudden squalls, like the shadow of a hand across the sea. Oh, for

281

weeks of this sort of life!"

An alternative to sailing was bathing naked in a small cove by the harbour mouth, with one of us keeping *cave* lest prowlers on the cliffs above should spot us. Afterwards lying prone on a rock, drying under the sun, the taste of salt upon our lips. "Sometimes my book comes so strongly on me that it's like a restless urge within saying 'Get on! Get on!' I want silence more than anything, the peace of solitude, long hours for reflection. A line from a poem by Emily Brontë has come to me clearly, and I shall call my book *The Loving Spirit*. This, I feel, is what I wish it to be. And always, no matter what people say to me, there must be Truth. No striving after cleverness, nor cheap and ready-made wit. Sincerity — beauty — purity."

Scrappy but endearing letters came from Carol almost every day — "Darling Daph, when are you coming back?" — although I told him in my own letters, time and time again, that I would stop down at Fowey after the others returned, because I wanted to get started on my book. He was busy anyway. Edgar's *The Calendar* had opened at Wyndham's and was a great success. Carol had a small part; he also stage-managed. He would understand that I must work, just as he must work. We would be together again when I had finished.

Ferryside suddenly seemed over-full of relatives. Great-aunts Finn and Blanche came to visit their niece M. What did it feel like to be old? "I saw their clothes on the spare-room beds. Grave hats high in the crown, and long dark warm 'wraps.' To think they were young once, and ran about gaily, and now walk with bent necks and hard stiff backs, not quite taking in what one says, and smiling vaguely to themselves. Aunt Finn mutters to herself under her breath 'Nonsense!' about nothing while Aunt Blanche continually misses the point and carries on with a topic of conversation that had ceased two minutes before. They're so funny, and yet . . ."

The last day of September came. In a couple of days everyone, including M and Angela, would have gone. The house was to be shut up, and it was arranged that I should lodge with Miss Roberts at The Nook, the cottage opposite. I could keep my bedroom at Ferryside open so as to write there during the day. But I would sleep, eat and live at The Nook, dear Bingo with me. No bathroom — Miss Roberts would fill a hip bath with hot water every morning — and the "usual office," as Geoffrey always called it, up the garden path. Who cared? I'd be on my own. And Miss Roberts, cheerful, smiling, gave Bingo and me a warm welcome, the first of many which would follow through the years to come. Dear Miss Roberts, who never looked askance at my shorts, or trousers, or muddy sea boots, who struggled upstairs each morning with her can of hot water, who pretended not to notice when, disliking sausages for supper, I furtively threw them on the sitting-room fire where they crackled loudly, and whose pleasant tittle-tattle of village gossip, invariably without malice, proved so entertaining.

It was strange to look across at Ferryside, bolted and shuttered, but I had a key, and went across the first morning, October 3rd, to the desk in my old bedroom, wrapped a rug around my knees, spread out sheets of paper and, filling my fountain pen, wrote in capital letters THE LOVING SPIRIT. Beneath it the lines from Emily Brontë's poem.

> Alas, the countless links are strong,
> That bind us to our clay,
> The loving spirit lingers long,
> And would not pass away.

The original Jane Slade should become Janet Coombe, Polruan across the harbour become Plyn, and Janet's loving spirit must endure through four generations. So, here goes.

''Such a step, this, as I took up my pen. It went fairly well and smoothly, though the writing of it is an entirely fresh style for me. There were no dire pauses and lapses of thought but a book of this sort mustn't rattle ahead. Weather right for starting too. A terrible wild day, with a howling sou'westerly wind and slashing rain. It doesn't matter a pin to me because it's all in tune with my writing. In fact it's a good thing, because I wasn't tempted to be out all the while."

I had soon settled down to a routine. Work in the morning, across to Miss Roberts' for lunch, then a pull down-harbour in *Annabelle Lee* in the afternoon or a tramp with Bingo. A cup of tea at The Nook, and back to work at Ferryside until it was time to pack up for the evening, and go back for supper at Miss Roberts'. Lamplight and candles in the sitting room, alone in privacy, with Miss Roberts "dishing up" my sups in the kitchen alongside, after which she would retire early to bed, and I would stretch myself on the small hard-backed sofa to read. The reading diet consisted chiefly of Mary Webb, lately discovered, and my uncrowned king of Fowey, the famous "Q." One of his novels, *Shining Ferry,* was all about my village of Bosinnick. How humble, even abashed, I should have felt then had I known that some thirty years later, dear Sir Arthur in his grave, his daughter Foy would ask me to complete the unfinished manuscript of the last novel her father ever wrote, *Castle Dor*. Nor was this the only link between the great man and myself. The title of my own novel published in 1941 — *Frenchman's Creek* — was not original: "Q" had used it many years before in one of his short stories, and graciously gave me permission to use it again, saying, if I remember rightly, that he looked forward to seeing what I had made of it, while adding a laughing though very genuine warning that "no critic would ever forgive me for the success of *Rebecca*." Truly a prophet! But in 1929 all that concerned me was the story of *The Loving Spirit*.

Work progressed well. I had finished Part One in a fortnight and Part Two by November 3rd, which, I told myself, was really good going.

"I don't think it's scrappy or carelessly done, at least I hope not. Anyway, I *felt* it all, which was of supreme importance. If only the hours were longer — I keep being aware of time slipping away. It was fun becoming Joseph, a man of 50 madly wanting his silly virgin of 19. I got so worked up over it all I could think of nothing else. I only snatched ¾ of an hour for exercise, and leapt up Hall Walk and round by the farm and back, but I could have gone on working all night. Can't help it if I get brain fever, I can't stop where I am now, it's too exciting. Blast, tomorrow I must do some letters or everyone will think me dead.''

Part Three would be more of a problem. The member of the third generation did not interest me as much as Janet and her son Joseph, and he also had to live in London for a while. I wished I had a history book, giving some details of the years 1888 - 1912. Word got around through Miss Roberts, and two days later Richard Bunt from Lamellon, ''up the hill and across the fields,'' appeared with an armful of superb volumes, profusely detailed and illustrated. ''Oh, the darling man. How terribly sweet to take the trouble. Oh, these are my people, they really are. What have I to do with London? I shall live and die here in Cornwall and do my best to write about them. What's the use of being clever and witty? It's a heart that is the needful thing. P.S. I wish I was a really good writer."

Many years later, after the war, myself married with three children, the same Richard Bunt would be skipper of the motor sailer *Fanny Rosa,* which my soldier husband would bring back from Singapore; but in the autumn of 1929 I did not even know that such a soldier existed.

November 1929, and I was still pegging away at Part Three, with a lump on my third finger from holding my pen too tightly. A pity I didn't own a typewriter. The autumn gales blew continuously but this never worried me, for I had brought the leading member of the third generation of my Slade-Coombe family back to Plyn, and the harder the wind blew the faster sped the story.

Sunday suppers with the Quiller-Couches became a routine, a happy relaxation after the week's work, and back at The Nook Miss Roberts' cheerful prattle proved an additional amusement. Tales of a former male lodger who had been "a little overindulgent" where alcohol was concerned, and although it was totally unconnected with this unfortunate gentleman, knowing my fondness for verse she produced a book of poems by a Mr. Postlethwaite which contained the lines,

O! rear no stone above my head,
Carve no Hic Jacet on my tomb.

I had an instant vision of the lodger reading these lines and spluttering Hic Jacet as he stumbled up the steps of The Nook en route from the Ferry Inn.

On Sunday, November 17th, I had finished Part Three, and laying aside the manuscript I went up to the hills above the harbour and listened to the church bells ringing for evensong from Lanteglos church, where my Jane was buried. It was a fitting climax. For in two days' time I was due back home at Hampstead, and there would be no more writing until after Christmas. A letter from M the day before I left contained a warning. ''I hope when you come home you won't start that practice of going out again in the evenings, which was so worrying." Really! It made me feel like a maid receiving reproof from the mistress of the house. Why did she not add, "Otherwise, we shall have to make a change"?

So I should have to sit every evening reading a book, Shakespeare or Dickens, and just accept it. It was the principle I minded, the knowledge that returning to Cannon Hall meant loss of freedom. Well, I was determined it would not be for long. Poor Bingo seemed to know, as I packed my suitcase. But Miss Roberts was going to look after him, so I had no worries on that score. And it seemed altogether right that I should leave on a wet, dismal day, the trees dank and lifeless; even Miss Roberts' macaw Rob, perched as usual on the sea wall, sat with his fine head humped between bedraggled feathers. But why, oh why, I asked myself, after the first family greeting, all smiles and how well I was looking, must I be the one to have restraint put upon my outings while Angela could do as she liked? "Whoopee ad lib, so she told me. Lord, how she made me laugh!"

Fortunately, there was no restriction put upon my days, and after a haircut and shampoo in London the first morning home I met Cousin Geoffrey for lunch. "He looked pale and tired, and showed, for the first time, little signs of fussiness and irritation. His good humour didn't bubble up as it used to do, in its old careless spontaneity. No job, which must be lowering to his whole outlook. And I've let him down terribly, I haven't helped him as I swore I always would. So lonely for him, living in rooms alone in Holland Road." He was forty-four, which, D always maintained, was the Du Maurier unlucky number. Perhaps Geoffrey would brighten up when he reached the lucky number forty-eight. But it seemed a fair time to wait.

I myself could not wait until five o'clock when I had a date with Carol at the Park Lane Hotel. "Oh, it was lovely to see him again. We sat in the lounge and drank orangeades, and talked for an hour. Then he drove me home, for me to be in time for dinner, and we stopped in Regent's Park for ten minutes because we simply had to kiss each other!''

Did I look guilty, I wonder, as, with hair patted into place and fresh lipstick added, I rushed down to the dining room as the gong sounded, all of forty-seven years ago? For such was to be the hurried routine, at least four days a week, until Christmas; and with D busy rehearsing to play Captain Hook, his old part, once more with Jean Forbes-Robertson as Peter Pan, there was no time for searching questions from Alexander Borgia. And Carol was busy too. He also had matinées and rehearsals, and was not always free, which meant days at Cannon Hall with little to do.

''The day has a thousand hours. Jeanne was out, Angela is away for the weekend, and M was busy doing the flowers. What good did I do anyone by moping upstairs in the schoolroom? It's the last time, I vow. I rang up Doodie, I rang up Dora, both were out. I tidied my desk and read Shakespeare, and it poured with rain. If I had been at Fowey there would have been peace. It's no use, I don't belong here.''

Why did I not offer to help M with the

flowers? Fear of a rebuff or total lack of interest? A chance, surely, for companionship, ignored by both of us. A mutual shyness between mother and daughter which would endure until after D died five years later, when, hearing the news by telephone, I hurried home and found her lying in bed, crying, and she put her arms round me and said, "He was so fond of you," and I held her close for the first time, and tried to comfort her. Twenty-five years too late. . . .

Christmas was to be spent at home, and at least the buying of presents kept me fully occupied. Especially the one for Carol.

"I'd known for months what to give him. I went to Hay's and bought him a gramophone — Columbia portable — with eight records in the lid. Then I went to the Park Lane Hotel, knowing he was out, and went up to his room and arranged it there, all open and ready, with a record on it. I looked at his things in the wardrobe. Poor sweet, he had no buttons on anything, nobody looks after his clothes. It's these sort of touches that make me love him."

On Boxing Day I heard the result of the Christmas gift. "I went to the Park Lane and found Carol waiting for me. He was absolutely thrilled with his gramophone, and he had found it exactly as I planned. I've never seen anyone so pleased. He was just like a little boy, all red in the face and smiling. We went upstairs and played it, then I sat with him while he had his dinner before the evening show. But I think I shall have the song of *Am I Blue?* in my head till my dying day."

Carol's present to me was a cigarette lighter, and a handsome fountain pen and pencil to match. Indeed, I did well that Christmas, with £5 from D, two sets of satin underwear from M, a bracelet from Angela, and handkerchiefs from Jeanne. Even dear out-of-work Geoffrey produced a diamond-paste necklace. While Michael Joseph from Curtis Brown, perhaps as subtle encouragement, sent me a work of his own entitled *Short Story Writing for Profit*. Thinking of the unfinished manuscript waiting for me down at Fowey I did not take the hint, and the last book of the year to be read on New Year's

Eve, after a family party skating on the ice rink at Golders Green, was *Good-bye to All That* by Robert Graves.

I awoke to despondency on January 1st, 1930. What if my novel turned out to be no good? "I have a sudden conviction that my book is not only dull but badly written, that it might as well be in the waste-paper basket." I shut myself up in the garage room and scribbled some articles in case Uncle Willie might think them worth publishing in *The Bystander*. At ten guineas apiece they would bring in thirty quid, and I could keep myself at Miss Roberts' for weeks on that. A letter from Fernande brought further despondency. She had actually been over to London before Christmas and had never told me. But why? What had I done to deserve such treatment? It wasn't fair. Fowey in a couple of days would be the only salvation. "Oh hell, if only one didn't care about anyone in the world. If only one could just laugh and be alone. I think of myself and how I live from week to week, from day to day, clutching at straws. I almost cried leaving Fowey some weeks ago, and this evening because I left Carol I had to put the newspaper in front of my face as I walked to the tube so as to hide the tears running down my cheeks. What in God's name does it mean? That I'm a bloody fool.''

So forget it, push it aside, and be on time to catch the train at Paddington. ''Once I arrived in Fowey, although it was dark, I saw the harbour thick with shipping, and the dark water gleaming, and Adams met me, and at the door of The Nook was Bingo, crazy with joy. Nothing changed since I left, the same identical piece of soap in the dish, surely the same candle. All as before. This was what I needed to reassure me. I might never have gone away, and yet something is changed somewhere, inside myself. Is it because I'm uncertain of my writing?''

Rain, sleet, wind, hail — *and* snow; I had hardly expected this from my Fowey. It was too cold to work at Ferryside, so I settled down in the sitting room at The Nook. But Part Four would not be easy. The last member of the four generations,

Jane Slade's great-granddaughter Jennifer, was going to be rather tiresome. I was not sure what to do with her. Could it be that I had lost interest in the whole story? If so, heaven help me. I snuggled down under my blanket in the mornings, hearing the rain against the window, and when a smiling Miss Roberts knocked on the door and brought in my can of hot water she said, "Why not stay where you are, Miss Daphne? After all, there is nothing for you to get up for, is there?"

Nothing to get up for . . . And she had been bustling around since six. It was shaming, with Part Four waiting untouched in the sitting room below.

"All right, Miss Roberts. I'll be down directly."

Then with the post a welcome letter from Curtis Brown saying *The Bystander* had accepted one of the articles, and would pay fifteen guineas. This was better. But as I pegged away at Part Four down in the sitting room Miss Roberts' quavering voice singing hymns in the kitchen across the hall put me off my stroke. Surely Katherine Mansfield would not have been so easily discouraged? Then came excitement. The rockets went off and the lifeboat was called out. The ferrymen told me there was a ship in distress off the Cannis Rock by Pridmouth. Too late to go and investigate now, but I would do so tomorrow.

"The day was fine, and after working like one possessed through the morning I crossed the Ferry after lunch and walked to Pridmouth. There she was, sure enough, right in the bay on the rocks, the sea breaking against her, and already her iron bottom torn open. I was told the crew had all got off safely. Ths sight was mournful. On one side, pathetic, and spars and driftwood cast on the shore. Even a magazine lying in a pool. People like busy flies on the beach scavenging."

The sight would remain in memory. Not for *The Loving Spirit,* but for another book, *Rebecca,* many years later, the seed as yet unsown.

I had completed three chapters of Part Four, and I had planned seven to come. One thing was certain. It would not be written in the style of a novel I had found on Miss Roberts' shelf called *Patricia of Pall Mall*. I couldn't forbear jotting a line from it in the diary, it made me laugh so much. " 'Plucky little girl,' he said tenderly, for her aloofness attracted him. Man-like, he preferred shy game." So now I knew how to behave. And perhaps if I wrote like that I should earn more than fifteen quid a story.

Meanwhile, news came from home that D, M and Angela were all off to Naples and then Capri for a three weeks' holiday. Good for them. I was not envious. I had only one plan, which was to finish the book, and Jennifer was turning out to be a hardheaded young woman, quite different from how I had intended her. This must surely mean I had no control over my characters.

A typist, employed by the famous "Q," arrived to carry off the first part of the book to type. I hoped she would be able to read my handwriting and wouldn't be too shocked at the spelling. I felt awkward giving it to her, thinking of all the faults and mistakes, the lame style, the somewhat indelicate expressions used from time to time. "I shan't look her in the eyes after she's read it. Then I washed my hair, and at once looked like a wild poet, frenzied, and in a decline. I met Mrs. Burghard on the ferry, who said to me, 'You don't look half so well as you did in the summer, you have got so skinny.' Thank you for nothing, Mrs. B." Supper with the Quiller-Couches restored morale. They were so friendly and sympathetic always, and their quiet humour was a real tonic.

A few days later Mrs. Smith brought back the first part typed. And hurrah! "She warmed my heart by telling me she found it so interesting she could hardly wait for Part Two! What's the betting she will be the first and last person ever to read it? However, her opinion did me good."

Thursday, January 30th. "At last! The final stroke has been drawn, the final word written, and *The Loving Spirit* is now finished. It has taken me exactly ten weeks, I calculate, which seems to me to be an extraordinarily quick piece of work when reckoned thus, and yet the labour has been enormous. There seems so much body in it, yet I don't know. I probably can't count, but I think it is over 200,000 words long! Oh God, that typing bill with Mrs. Smith. The relief to have done it, though, is enormous. I was so excited I could hardly eat my lunch. In the afternoon I went over to Lanteglos church to make some sort of thanksgiving, and to visit the tombstone of Jane Slade. If Michael Joseph of Curtis Brown tells me he doesn't like it, or I must rewrite, he can go to hell. I can't go back to it any more.

"The future faces me with doubt and perplexity. 'No coward soul is mine'?"

I knew instinctively that now my work was done reaction would set in, even in beloved Fowey. Even to glance through the manuscript made me feel dull and stale. The family still in Capri, except for Jeanne at school in Hampstead, I could snatch several evenings with Carol before they returned, without the inevitable disapproval. Besides, it was raining heavily. Trudging along Hall Walk above Bodinnick was like ploughing through Flanders mud. I took my manuscript over to good Mrs. Smith the typist and left it with her, with instructions to post it all back to me at Cannon Hall when her work was completed, and on February 4th I left for London.

But disenchantment continued. Carol had a heavy cold, and was busy rehearsing. An aching tooth sent me to the dentist, who pronounced that the nerve was dying. How incredibly dreary everything seemed to be! I pottered about at home and discovered an old diary of my grandfather's written in 1867, and became fascinated by his changing moods. Yes, perhaps we *were* alike. Yet in 1867 he was thirty-three, and now in 1930 I was still only twenty-two. As soon as the family returned from Capri I would be off to Paris, *pour changer les idées* as Fernande would say. Besides, I felt guilty that I had not yet stayed in the new house at Neuilly.

On February 22nd — when the family had been home a week, full of the delights of Capri — my typed manuscript came back from Mrs. Smith. "I have never seen such a stupendous parcel. It looked like a huge package from the laundry, almost too ridiculous to be impressive. I shut myself up in the garage-room and got through most of it during the day, working hard all the time. I can now decide to go to Paris next Monday, and will get someone to drop it in with Michael Joseph at Curtis Brown. I go down to the Park Lane Hotel and tell Carol about Paris. He didn't really want me to go at first, but afterwards agreed that anyway the next month will be hopeless as regards 'us,' as he has all these rehearsals. I do hope he won't work too hard. Good-bye again."

Once in Paris the spirits rose. The house was lovely, though somewhat lacking the homely atmosphere of the little one in Boulogne-sur-Seine. For one thing it was a real finishing school, with a crowd of girls I had never seen. Three Belgians, one Norwegian, a Hungarian, and the rest English. Also visiting daily teachers shouting all over the place. Fernande in a good mood, but working far too hard.

"Still, the smell of Paris is always the same, wherever you go, and the bright tingly air. Men in working clothes on bicycles, sitting over their *déjeuner* in cafés with *Tabac* written above. And there is a market in the Avenue de Neuilly, full of gruyère cheeses and *légumes,* and things one longs to put in a *panier,* and Jews selling silks, old people passing, and three marvellous Africans dressed in their native clothes — one very tall, quite young, in white, with a purple turban. When I got back there was a letter from Michael Joseph, who had read the book and liked it very much. That's one load off my mind. Of course, whether Mr. Evans of Heinemann likes it is another matter.''

Not much good news from home. An article I had written for *The Bystander* before Christmas, entitled ''Our Elders and Betters,'' had been published, and everybody was shocked! Godmother Billy was horrified. True, I had mocked at the older generation, but with tongue in cheek. Couldn't they see the fun of it? Apparently not. Oh dear, I could do nothing right.

Never mind, an afternoon with Fernande on the *rive gauche* and tea at the Café du Dome at Montparnasse restored my gaiety. "I could pass my days here at a table, watching, watching the faces of the people. The trees are beginning to bud, but they look too confident of promise under the grey light and the grey skies. The bark of the trees is black. Taxis hooted. Somewhere there is a story singing in my ears, 'I'll Never Be Young Again . . . I'll Never Be Young Again.' But it won't be born yet awhile."

On March 30th, exactly two months to the day after I had finished *The Loving Spirit* at Fowey, a letter came from Michael Joseph to say that Heinemann had accepted the book, both for England and for America. It was too long and would have to be cut, which I could do myself when I returned to London — he would show me how it was done. Simply crossing through certain paragraphs of my own choice which did not contribute either to characterisation or to the story. No rewriting would be necessary. As to the date of publication, Charlie Evans of Heinemann had no immediate plan, and it very well might be they would hold it over now — with their autumn list prepared — until after Christmas. It would mean better sales.

"Wonderful news," I reported in the diary, "and I am so pleased." As to the possible holdup of publication, well, it would be a bore to have the book hanging about, but it couldn't be helped, and during the summer I could start on No. 2. The boy who ran away to sea was simmering there, not nineteenth-century like *The Loving Spirit* but present-day, young, the same age as Carol and myself, and later he would come to live in Paris, in the Rue du Cherche Midi.

A few more days left before going back home. "I sat by the open window at Neuilly, and gave my thoughts up to complete negation of active thinking, which is what I subconsciously call working. Some weeks hence the ideas that come into my head without my knowledge today will begin to open and unfold, like the leaves on the trees here that have begun too early. Creation is the same in every way."

One of the first things I did when I

returned was to go along to Michael Joseph's house and meet his wife and children, and then we set to work on *The Loving Spirit* typescript. He showed me how to cut, and I understood fully the reason for it, taking it back home to finish in the garage room. "No sentimentality about this job. I was ruthless, and crossed out passages that had given me exquisite pleasure to write. But it teaches me a hell of a lot, and does me no end of good for the future. I worked at it without a break except for meals. Michael won't be able to say I haven't done it thoroughly, and I'm sure it's made a terrific difference for the better."

So that was that. Dispatched to Michael and from him to Heinemann, and I could banish the whole business from my mind until the book was published.

To Fowey immediately afterwards, a blessed interlude through April and May, with a riding expedition to the Lizard with Foy Quiller-Couch thrown in for good measure, and then work began on the new book, *I'll Never Be Young Again*. No garage room at home for this, but permission to use Godmother Billy's secretarial office in Orange Street, off Leicester Square, where she put an extra room at my disposal. "Lovely, darling, to have you come down with me every day and write, I shall enjoy it." Yes, and so would I, nipping out to lunch at the Café Anglais with Carol. No one could object to that.

My work progressed so well that the book was finished in a couple of months, and I wrote the last line — the words of the title — on July 18th. "I stayed all alone at the office until nine in the evening, when it was done. I had a queer dinner all by myself at Lyons café. [Carol was away.] Then I came home in the tube. Now for reaction. I'm so tired."

It was strange to have a second book completed and the first not yet published. Stranger still to go on holiday to Brittany with Fernande a fortnight later, staying in Quimper, and make an excursion to the Pointe du Raz and the Baie des Trépassés, which I had written about in *I'll Never Be Young Again* and never seen, to find it just as I had described. So that was where poor Jake was drowned, that was where the narrator, the boy Dick, swam ashore. "I sat there alone, and I saw the waves shatter themselves upon the ship, and I watched the rain fall into the sea, and the grey dawn breaking." That was Dick, in the book, but in the diary, two months later, it was myself staring down at the Baie des Trépassés. "I knew it would be like this. Wild rocks, and the sea breaking below. The same mist that later lifted. It was wonderful." Not quite so wonderful, but rather more sinister, to learn, when I was in Fowey at the end of August, that a yacht had drifted on to the rocks in Lantivit Bay and six people had been drowned, the debris with their bodies drifting ashore. I seemed to be haunted by shipwreck. "Another body had been found in Lantivit Bay. There is something queerly allied in all this to my story, and the Baie des Trépassés. Yet mine came first."

There was nothing to draw me back to London for three glorious months. Carol was in America; so sailing, swimming and walking became the order of the day.

310

The Quiller-Couches suggested that I should write to the owner of Menabilly, Dr. Rashleigh, and ask permission to wander in the grounds, which I did, though I discreetly refrained from climbing in at a back window when permission was granted. In November Foy Quiller-Couch and I went on another riding expedition, this time to Bodmin moors, putting up at the wayside hostelry, Jamaica Inn. It was my first sight of the place that would later grip my imagination almost as much as Menabilly. A temperance house in 1930, it had been a coaching stop in old days, and I thought of the travellers in the past who must have sought shelter there on wild November nights, watched by the local moorland folk. No temperance house then, but a bar where the little parlour was, the drinking deep and long, fights breaking out, the sound of oaths, men falling.

"In the afternoon we ventured out across the moors," I noted in the diary, "desolate, sinister, and foolishly lost our way. To our horror rain and darkness fell upon us, and there we were, exposed to the violence of night with scarcely a hope of returning. Struck what we thought was a farm, but it was only a derelict barn. I was for staying, but Foy said we would catch our death. Blindly, helplessly, we let the reins lie loosely on the necks of the horses, and they led us back in the direction from which we had come, and by a miracle we saw in the distance the light from Jamaica Inn. All thanks to the instinct of the horses. Sat weary to supper but immeasurably happy. If only instead of one night I could spend days here."

I should in a later year, in person and in fancy, but not yet.

A cheque for £67 had already arrived from Heinemann via Curtis Brown, the advance for *The Loving Spirit,* and very welcome it was too. It was the largest cheque I had ever received. But oh dear, it was going to be the usual wrench leaving Miss Roberts and Bingo, where I had been happily installed since the family went back in October. And Miss Roberts was so brave. One evening she spilt a kettle of boiling water over her legs, scalding them terribly, and I would have known nothing about it but for the fact that she called to me from the kitchen, ''I am afraid your supper may be a little late, Miss Daphne,'' and I went to her, and she was sitting there with long strips of skin falling from her knees.

Other friends I would miss were Adams, dear Richard Bunt and his wife, old Mr. Phelps, a friend of the ''Q's'' — with whom I used to have tea, and he invariably walked me back to the Ferry after Sunday supper at The Haven— a bedridden Dr. Cann, Miss Alice Rashleigh, who told me stories about Menabilly and had lived there as a girl. All these people I was fond of, and the older they were the more endearing.

''Pages could be written about today. The mist in the morning, and the sun in a blaze of light about a lane shining through a spider's web, through a last leaf, on rich earth. And the afternoon, cooler, sharper, but the hills strangely alive, and when evening came the sky was pale crimson, blotting out into mist and fog like inked paper. Cattle noises in the distance.

Children calling." Good-bye, good-bye, everyone, and back to London.

Christmas at Hampstead, holly and mistletoe, a large family gathering with additional friends, even a conjurer to entertain us, and before the day itself a few snatched encounters with Carol, home from America and busy rehearsing yet another play. His present to me a cigarette case, inside which he had scribbled in pencil "Daph from Carol." I have it to this day, forty-six years later, the pencil marks just legible.

Paris in the New Year, and wandering about the market in the Avenue de Neuilly the idea for book No. 3 rose to the surface. No ships, no wrecks, no boys running away to sea. The life story of a French Jew — his name would be Julius Lévy. I saw his grandfather, and his mother, and their humble surroundings in Puteaux across the Seine. I saw him as an old man first, dying, and then as a child. I must follow him throughout his life. Where on earth had he sprung from into my mind? I didn't know. He was there. He was suddenly alive. "It doesn't matter if this takes a year, I shall not hurry," I wrote on February 7th, "but his early life spans the 1870 war between France and Prussia. I won't shrink from it. I won't. I must look up all the history of the siege of Paris and the Fourth of September. I must work like fury."

A letter from Michael Joseph informed me that *The Loving Spirit* would be published on February 23rd. "They are boring to have kept it back so long," I noted, "and I bet there won't be any reviews of it. Anyway, I'm working on my 3rd now."

Then D telephoned. He had received an advance copy. "He liked it very much. It was nice to hear that. I had a feeling he would never get through it. He says he is going away for a week to look at birds in Norfolk. Quite mad."

February 23rd. "Worked hard all the morning, and then caught the 4 o'clock train to London. D and M away for a week. By the way, my book came out today."

So . . . I had been launched, just as the schooner *Jane Slade* had been launched by her namesake in the last century. How long I would remain afloat depended upon the rocks and shoals, fair weather or foul, that I might find in the seas ahead, not forgetting my own skill as a helmsman, which would come with practice. One thing was certain: the advance on royalty payments, from Heinemann in London and Doubleday, Doran & Company in New York, assured me that I could henceforward maintain myself, whether in Fowey, Paris or elsewhere, though naturally I should live at Cannon Hall with the family whenever I chose to return to London. Independence. Freedom. No ties.

News note sent to 600 papers from Doubleday, Doran & Company, Inc., Garden City, New York: Daphne du Maurier's novel, *The Loving Spirit,* which Doubleday, Doran will publish in July, is receiving enthusiastic praise from Rebecca West, Robert Lynd, Gerald Gould and other English critics. Miss du Maurier is the daughter of the actor Gerald du Maurier and granddaughter of George du Maurier, who wrote *Trilby* and *Peter Ibbetson."*

"The Loving Spirit is a fine, widely sweeping romance of family life over four generations, of strong sentiment, lively episodes, Cornish locality, sea-life, and domestic vicissitudes." *The Times*

"Miss du Maurier creates on the grand scale; she runs through the generations, giving her family unity and reality . . . a rich vein of humour and satire . . . observation, sympathy, courage, a sense of the romantic, are here." *The Observer*

"The narrative flows smoothly and easily, while in the figures of Janet, Joseph and Jennifer the wild, eerie spirit that urges them beyond all prudence and obedience is represented in episodes and descriptions of considerable power." *Times Literary Supplement*

So my book had been published, yet

somehow I couldn't feel excited about it. It belonged to the mood of 1929, when I wrote out the title *The Loving Spirit* on a blank page, and then turned to the next page, and wrote at the top of it "Chapter One." Two autumns ago. Then the story was alive within me, burning to be written, and now it was something confined between hard covers that other people would read, borrowing it from W. H. Smith or forking out seven and sixpence if they felt so inclined. It was not mine any more.

I'll Never Be Young Again, more recent, like a newborn child, waited on the stocks for when Heinemann chose to publish, while, Julius, my Julius, who "stretched out his arms to the sky," his first and his last gesture, was milling around in my head. I *must* start working upon him, but impossible in London.

The mood of disenchantment increased, made more intensive by a severe cold, followed immediately by a second. The news from Mr. Evans of Heinemann that *The Loving Spirit* had gone into a second edition was pleasant but conveyed little, and when someone from a newspaper came up to Cannon Hall to photograph me I felt a fool. Was this the sort of thing most writers enjoyed?

The cold temporarily conquered, I accepted an invitation from my American publisher, Nelson Doubleday, to an evening party at the Embassy, full of swells like Brigadier Spears and Mary Borden, Helen Simpson, Michael and Atalanta Arlen, and though I enjoyed the novelty I felt out of place. It was not, as they say today, "my scene." Carol was in Berlin, seeing about some play of Edgar's, and Geoffrey, with whom I lunched about now, irritated me for the first time in my life by being offensive to a waiter in the restaurant, criticising the poor service. Did he think to impress me? The reverse.

No, I must get down to Fowey. Fowey would be my salvation. I sent a telegram to dear Miss Roberts telling her to expect me on the twenty-seventh. And when I arrived, to be met by Adams and a smiling Miss Roberts, with Bingo wagging his tail, I wrote at the top of the diary, referring to what I had left behind me,

"Good-bye to All That."

Good-bye indeed. I did not return to London until the autumn. The family, of course, came down for Easter, and again in August, but between times I was blissfully alone, dividing my time between working on my Jewish Julius, digging and hacking in the Ferryside garden, walking Bingo, sailing *Marie-Louise,* and once a week having Sunday supper with the Quiller-Couches.

"Sir Arthur sweet about my book," the diary says, "and his is the only criticism worth a damn." Perhaps it is worth reminding myself that he was not so favourably inclined to book No. 2, *I'll Never Be Young Again,* which I fear he found a little shocking, bless his heart.

There were expeditions, too, with his daughter Foy. The Helford River in pony and jingle, plus a tent, and later in the year a second jaunt to the Bodmin moors and a couple of nights at Jamaica Inn. This time we did not lose ourselves, although it was mid-November and pouring wet; I remember reading *Treasure Island* over a peat fire, and something must have stirred within me, to come to life again in after years, especially as we visited the neighbouring village and fine church at Altarnun, and surprisingly a little parson called upon us during the evening. What seed was dropped that night into the subconscious? I shall never know.

I rather overdid things in the Ferryside garden that autumn. Felling trees and sawing wood brought on pains in the side and nausea, both heralding a mild attack of appendicitis, which I did not realise at the time but would know about later, in the New Year. On November 25th I finished my novel about Julius. It had taken me nine months, and the diary says, "All the labour of having a child. I drank its health in sloe gin!" Little did I know that in exactly twelve months' time I should be one month pregnant with my own live baby — my future daughter Tessa; and had some fortuneteller read my hand at that moment in 1931 I would have laughed the seer to scorn. Growing pains over, I was about to become mature.

In the late summer of 1931, or it may have been in the early autumn, before sawing down trees gave me those warning signals of impending appendicitis, a thirty-five-year-old major in the Grenadier Guards, Boy Browning to his brother officers, second in command to the second battalion of his regiment, said to one of his closest friends in the Grenadiers, "I've read a novel called *The Loving Spirit,* one of the best books I've read for years, and apparently it's all about Fowey in Cornwall. I'm determined to go down there in my boat *Ygdrasil,* and see the place for myself. Perhaps I'll have the luck to meet the girl who has written it. How about it? Will you come with me?" John Prescott, the brother officer, agreed, and together they proceeded down the coast and arrived in Fowey. It was Sister Angela who first spotted them.

"There's a most attractive man going up and down the harbour in a white motorboat," she said, watching through field glasses from the hatch window at Ferryside. "Do come and look."

Mildly interested, I obeyed the summons. "H'm," I said, "he *is* rather good."

The cruising up and down continued through the week, and some local gossip informed us that the stunning helmsman was called Browning, and he was said to be the youngest major in the British army! And that was that. I thought no more about him.

It was not until the following year, 1932, in April, having survived my mild operation for appendicitis, and arriving down in my beloved Fowey to recuperate, that I heard "Major Browning" was in the harbour and afloat again, having laid up his boat *Ygdrasil* with the Bodinnick boatbuilder, one of my neighbours, George Hunkin.

Mrs. Hunkin was my informant. "The major would like to meet you," she told me. "He's very nice."

"Oh?"

I was secretly flattered, and to attract attention had my pram up on the slipway and gave her a coat of varnish. A note in the current diary, on April 6th, says,

"That Browning man kept passing in his boat, but didn't attempt to do anything. Don't blame him. I sat around and read." (The current book was Aldous Huxley's *Brave New World*.)

The following day a note was brought to me by Mrs. Hunkin, which, though alas I never kept it, read as follows, to the best of my belief: "Dear Miss du Maurier, I believe my late father, Freddie Browning, used to know yours, as fellow-members of the Garrick Club. The Hunkins tell me you have had your appendix out and can't do much rowing yet, so I wondered if you would care to come out in my boat? How about tomorrow afternoon?" I sent word back that I should be delighted.

Friday, April 8th. "A fine bright day with a cold wind. In the afternoon I went out with Browning in his boat. It was the most terrific fun, the seas short and jumpy, and he put his boat hard into it, and we got drenched with spray. She's called *Ygdrasil* because he's mad on Norse mythology, and it means the Tree of Fate. His friends call him Boy, but he told me to call him Tommy, which is what his family call him. He's the most amazing person to be with, no effort at all, and I feel I've known him for years. I also showed him all over *Marie-Louise,* and then we came back, sat over a roaring fire which I lit, talked about everything in the world, and it was the most extraordinary evening I've ever spent."

The Tree of Fate . . . The next two days we spent entirely in each other's company, then he had to return to his battalion, but in a week he was back again, having driven through the night! I was sawing up some logs early in the morning, and I heard him call to Bingo. Hatless, brown leather jerkin, grey flannel trousers thrust into sea boots . . . green eyes, and a smile that curled at one corner. Yes, no doubt about it, he *was* good.

"You seem to get a lot of leave," I told him.

"Not much going on at the moment," he said, "and my commanding officer enjoys doing all the work. Besides, he happens to be one of my closest friends. Come on.

Leave those logs, *Yggy* is waiting for you."

I had never been given a direct order before, and I loved it! So the rapid courtship began, and MYSELF WHEN YOUNG is not the place to describe it. The past lay behind me. Enough to say that within a few weeks he became as much wedded to Fowey, the harbour, the river, the walks, the people, as I was myself. By the end of June, after frequent visits, we decided to become engaged, and we composed letters to our respective families, while he had to obtain official permission from his commanding officer. I also had to break the news to Carol.

Throwing the proverbial cap over the mill, we caught a midnight train and went to Purbright, where his battalion was stationed. I must meet his mother. "Sweet and kind," the diary says, "and his sister Grace such a good sort. Happy family atmosphere. I shall enjoy staying with them. It's all like a dream, and sometimes I feel I am a ghost with a path laid out before me, and a picture of every moment." This was July 2nd. On Sunday

326

the sixth we drove up to Hampstead. "Bit of a strain, of course. But D and M say we can have the cottage at the bottom of the garden at Cannon Hall, which is a wonderful solution to the dreadful London problem, where of course we shall have to live most of the time when he is on duty there."

D had apparently burst into tears when he first read my letter telling them I was engaged, and said, "It isn't fair." Then he became reconciled, because "brother Guy had been a soldier, and would have approved of a young officer who had won his D.S.O. as a subaltern in the war as well as the Croix de Guerre." M smiled and was sympathetic, and began talking about plans for the wedding, only to be disappointed when I told them both, "Oh, no, nothing big. Down at Fowey, at Lanteglos church, where Jane Slade was buried. Early in the morning. We can go by boat. Just yourselves, as Angela and Jeanne are away, and the Hunkins as witnesses."

It was a relief that Tommy felt as strongly about this decision as I did myself. By boat it must be, like the young couple in *The Loving Spirit*. And if all his friends expected a great do at the Guards' Chapel, well, bad luck for them. And so it was arranged. The engagement was announced. Letters of congratulation poured in, and I kept wishing the fuss could be over, we could just get married and disappear; then everyone would forget us.

Nerves on both our parts increased as the day drew near. I felt in a dither, as I had done before having my appendix out, and Tommy, despite that wartime D.S.O., was white about the gills and said he had chronic indigestion. D was silent, and Geoffrey — who had offered his services as best man to Tommy — made the usual jokes, which fell rather flat. M alone was superbly calm, and carefully ironed my faded blue coat and skirt the night before the wedding. "Whatever happens," I wrote in my diary that evening, "I want to remember that I am doing this with my eyes open, and because I want a fuller life, greater knowledge, and understanding. So adieu . . . Daphne du

Maurier." A fuller life . . . yes, for henceforward I would come to know what it was to love a man who was my husband, not a son, not a brother.

The sun shone for us the next day, July 19th. Time 8:15 A.M., so nobody was about. D, M, Geoffrey and I proceeded in the *Cora Ann* up Pont hill to Lanteglos. Tommy and the Hunkins followed in *Ygdrasil*.

"All very simple," I recorded, "quickly over. And afterwards Mrs. Hunkin called me Mrs. Browning, which sounded so strange. When we got back to the harbour everyone seemed to know what had happened, and people were waving from houses and cottages. We quickly had breakfast, then loaded stores on to *Yggy*, and set off for the harbour mouth and the open sea. The Quiller-Couches, in their rowing-boat, hailed us and presented a bottle of their home-brewed sloe gin. Then we were away, heading down-channel for Falmouth and the Helford River. We couldn't have chosen anything more beautiful."

The publishers hope that this Large Print Book has brought you pleasurable reading. Each title is designed to make the text as easy to see as possible. G. K. Hall Large Print Books are available from your library or local bookstore or through the Large Print Book Club. If you would like a complete list of the Large Print Books we have published or information about our Book Club, please write directly to:

G. K. Hall & Co.
70 Lincoln Street
Boston, Mass. 02111